M000002316

PRAISE FOR
Unboxed

Tomorrow's church looks and feels much different from yesterday's church. The message remains unchanging; however, the methods are ever growing and adjusting to futuring realities. In *Unboxed*, Martijn van Tilborgh challenges you to be curious about the future, and become an explorer to discover new lands and fresh opportunities. Unbox yourself, your leaders, and your church.

— Sam Chand
Leadership Consultant
Best-Selling Author
Atlanta, Georgia

In *Unboxed*, Martijn van Tilborgh, one of God's catalytic agents for getting us out of our comfort zones, takes us on a journey to release us from boxes we have lived in that imprison the greatness of Christ from being expressed through us. Martijn takes you through his own unboxing experience at the hand of a loving and caring Father and into the journey of a grand adventure of kingdom living. It is there that paradigm-breaking and paradigm-shattering moments lead us to open-ended rather than closed-ended futures where our expectations are no longer limited but, rather, limitless. Allow this stellar, prophetic, kingdom entrepreneur to take you on a Spirit-led journey. It will take you where there are possibilities that will collapse the false boundaries of the limited boxes you have been living in. It will take you where there is unboxed liberty and freedom as a son or daughter of God that is your birthright. Martijn's five keys to becoming unboxed, when applied, will change the trajectory of your life in more ways than you can imagine. Enjoy being unboxed!

— *Dr. Mark J. Chironna*
Pastor, Church On The Living Edge
Longwood, Florida

Regardless of whether the prophetic message came through the peculiarities of John the Baptist, the enigmatic ways of Ezekiel, or the youth and perceived immaturity of Jeremiah, what's unmistakable and undeniable is the significance of what God gave them to share with others. God has done it again through Martijn van Tilborgh. Without a doubt, *Unboxed* is God's prophetic voice, and Martijn is His vessel. This book is one that leaders and the church desperately need. And true to 2 Peter 1:19, this message is "light that shines brightly in the midst of darkness." Prepare to be challenged, changed, and empowered!

— Van Moody
Bestselling Author, Leadership Architect, Pastor
Birmingham, Alabama

I have had the privilege of working closely with Martijn for several years. He is an innovator, a strategist, and a man of God. Each conversation I have with Martijn results in my being stretched and challenged to think differently. Reading *Unboxed* will help you become the innovative person God has designed you to be!

— Brian Dollar
Kids Pastor, Author, I Blew It! and Talk Now and Later
Founder, HVK Ministry Resources
Little Rock, Arkansas

In this book, Martijn takes us on a journey. Knowing Martijn, I can assure you that it's his very own journey. Martijn and his family are now living the life that he could see in the Spirit long before it manifested in the natural. This book is about the journey that made it happen. It took supernatural courage and extreme willingness for them to literally leave behind everything they had and knew. *Unboxed* will challenge you and help you step into the exciting process of being unboxed! It is a process that will help you to discover the kingdom way of being the church of Jesus Christ in the earth.

— *Klaas van Denderen*
President, Founder, Father's House Ministries
Amsterdam, The Netherlands

Once in a blue moon there are books that come along that stop me in my tracks. *Unboxed* is one of those books. I couldn't stop reading it. This is more than a book; it's a paradigm shift that will reprogram the GPS of your organization's future. Get ready to highlight; underline; and, most importantly, move into action. If you been boxed in long enough, then this is your invitation to get unboxed once and for all.

— *Simon T. Bailey*
Leader, The Brilliance Movement
Windermere, Florida

Unboxed carves a path through the paradigms of our faith to brilliantly lead readers into the greater, richer life we've been called to. Through transparent conversations of revelation and biblical insight, Martijn challenges readers to journey out of life's limiting boxes and step into the unlimited possibilities of God. More than simply a book,

Unboxed will be your manual of transformation and change that beckons you to break out and live unboxed!

— Sergio De La Mora
Lead Pastor, Cornerstone Church of San Diego
Author, The Heart Revolution and Paradox
San Diego, California

"Boxes kill dreams." That one statement by author Martijn van Tilborgh in his new book, *Unboxed*, along with the coinciding stories and principles from this book, will help you look at your life with fresh perspective and possibilities. *Unboxed* is full of hope, inspiration and the challenge to move your life forward in a big way.

— Mike Lukaszewski
Entrepreneur, Consultant, Speaker
Atlanta, Georgia

Unboxed will take you from having potential to realizing your potential. Martijn is a masterful inspirational storyteller, yet he also gives you the step-by-step process necessary to break free from your current paradigms and be everything God has called you to be. His words of wisdom will help you radically grow the most important areas of your life. Personally, he has helped me to successfully launch and grow companies that are reaching people all over the world in ways I could never have imagined in my old "box."

— Dr. Ben Lerner
Founder, The Ultimate Impact Group
U.S. World Team Doctor
New York Times Bestselling Author
Windermere, Florida

This is a must-read for every pastor and Christian. Martijn challenges you to think differently about how and why you "do" church. The information contained in this book is foundational, biblical, and critical for today. Put this book at the top of your reading list!

— Ryan Frank
President, KidzMatter® magazine
Author, Speaker, Entrepreneur
Marion, Indiana

This excellent message and clear teaching is in total harmony with what God is speaking to me.

— Erik Erikson
Founder, President, The Gospel Channel
Reykjavik, Iceland

We can learn great lessons from points of personal pain. If we are wise, we can also learn from another's pain if they share those lessons with us. In *Unboxed*, Martijn shares with us not only lessons from pain but also how God has worked in his life to show him how to turn those lessons into kingdom advance. I encourage you to use this practical, hope-filled account to benefit your own life and work.

— *Dave Travis*
Former CEO, Leadership Network
Atlanta, Georgia

Unboxed is a book every church leader needs to get and read. Your old way of thinking and doing will be challenged so that you can break out of the old and into the new.

— *Benny Perez*
Lead Pastor, www.thechurchlv.com
Las Vegas, Nevada

Warning: Do not pick up this book if you are content with the status quo! In *Unboxed*, Martijn creates a blueprint we can follow to shift our mindset from the prison of what has always been to what is possible in God's limitless economy. Martijn, in his thought-provoking way, forces us to take the blinders off and really see where our thoughts, plans, and goals have been limited by in-the-box thinking. He then lays out an action plan for relevant, life-changing, awe-inspiring ways to do and love radical kingdom-building!

— *Beth Frank*
Creative Director, KidzMatter® magazine
Marion, Indiana

Unboxed is a remarkably insightful book written by one of the most lucid minds in the country. It will challenge you to leave your comfort zone and inspire you to live where the real adventure is—outside the box. If you want to be everything God intended you to be, then follow the practical wisdom of a thought leader who has successfully escaped the confines of his own box.

— *Zoro*
world-renowned Drummer
Author, Soar: 9 Proven Keys for Unlocking Your
Limitless Potential
Los Angeles, California

If ever a book title fit the perfect description of its author, it would be *Unboxed*! Martijn's unconventional, unorthodox business genius has not only been an inspiration to me but also the secret to his success and the success he has brought to others. The story behind *Unboxed* is one of a road less-traveled yet essential for the growth of any aspiring leader. Martijn's life compels us to realize that the "box" is the only thing that keeps us from fulfilling our full potential.

— *Erik Lindamood*
Precious Metals Monetization Director / Partner,
Barksanem Inc.
Nines, France

If you're tired of living an average life, and your heart longs for more, then get ready to stretch beyond what's familiar and comfortable to you. Martijn challenges us with *Unboxed* not only to think outside the box, but also to live outside every box that may be holding us captive and keeping us from living the abundant life we were created to live. He offers us a strategic step-by-step plan of action that is practical yet profound. It requires some work on our part, but it's necessary to doing life differently. For those with an insatiable appetite for more, *Unboxed* will inspire you to rise to new heights of revelation so you can discover who you are and fulfill the prophetic destiny God has planned for you. *Unboxed* does for the mind what a gym does for the body. You're in for a good workout!

— *Kathy R. Green*
Author, Speaker, Consultant, KRG Publications LLC
Flower Mound, Texas

Unboxed contains unique and refreshing revelations that could only have been given to Martijn by the Holy Spirit for this era. This book will help anyone who is seeking fulfillment, purpose, and destiny. Some of the insights, such as the need to shift our thinking as a method of bringing innovative solutions to human problems, are applicable not just in church or ministry settings but also in every realm of society. Martijn masterfully explores out-of-the-box thinking and gives it practical application.

— *Ayodeji Ani*
Entrepreneur
Lagos, Nigeria

Martijn challenges the boxes we have created in ministry and leadership through our "church" paradigm. He brings us back to the kingdom mindset we need in order to be most effective in our worlds. His heart is to shake leaders and ministries out of their limitations by showing us God's perspective on these issues so we can accomplish the best for our King. *Unboxed* maps out a journey every ministry needs to take.

— *Shaun Smit*
Leadership Mentor, Wonderful Leaders
Maidstone, United Kingdom

I have known Martijn more than twenty tears and I am excited about his book! *Unboxed* deals with mindsets, paradigms, culture, thought processes, and personal development and shows you how to get out of your personal box. Making an inventory of your belief system in order to help you identify the box you're in is a scary thing, but so necessary. We need courage to ask questions all the time, yet without any fear, trusting our covenant with Jesus and being assured of His love for us. But, in the end, a constant renewal of the mind is inevitable for us to live a life without limitations—unboxed!

— A.A. (Dolf) de Voogd van der Straaten
Vlissingen, The Netherlands

If you feel like your life is too small for what God wants to do in and through you, this book is a must-have. Through personal testimony and keen insight, my friend Martijn van Tilborgh prepares you to take a journey of discovery to fulfill beyond your life imagination. Prepare to live life like you have never known it before!

— Jeff Scott Smith
President, JSS Consulting Inc.
Pastor, Strong Tower Church
Fredericksburg, Virginia

Martijn does an amazing job of challenging us to get unboxed! More importantly, I love the way he continually points to Scripture and biblical examples to encourage us to start thinking differently.

— *David Laflin*
Internationally Recognized Christian Illusionist
Denver, Colorado

I highly recommend *Unboxed*. Why? Because I love reading books that invite me to be a part of the story and encourage me in my life of faith. I love reading books about what the writer has lived through. I love reading books that bring apostolic clarity about the finished work of Jesus and the kingdom of God, especially when the writer writes about what he sees in the Spirit. Blessings are unboxed in this book! Martijn is a dear friend, and from our first meeting it has been like "iron sharpening iron"—and that is exactly what *Unboxed* will do for you, dear reader.

— *Hilmar Kristinsson*
Theologian
Co-Founder, IAM / Iceland Apostolic Mission
Reykjavík, Iceland

I thoroughly enjoyed this incredible book. It has caused me to prayerfully unbox myself from the limitations I had subconsciously placed on myself. Many leaders in the kingdom, both in ministry and the marketplace, will benefit from this message, as it serves as an eye-opener to see beyond your current circumstance. My prayer is that many will be inspired the same way I have been inspired by reading it. *Unboxed* will allow you to see ancient truth within a new paradigm. This is a prophetic message written with intent for such a time as this!

— *Arie Tempelman*
Entrepreneur, Coach, Adviser
Vlissingen, The Netherlands

I am a fervent student of information. And sometimes information comes your way that has the inherent power to induce a radical wake-up slap on the inside of you. This is exactly the effect *Unboxed* produces. If you have ever felt like something in your life has to change but you can't put it into words, then you must read this book! In chapter after chapter, beams of light flooded my understanding about why, and most importantly how, to make a shift from the limited default positions we find ourselves in every day—or as Martijn labels it, the "box." I applaud the clarity and practicality of this work as well as the rich challenge Martijn issues for forward movement. Allow this book to identify your limitations and then to lead you out of the box—and most of all, let it teach you how to create a whole new reality in your life.

— *Dr. Romero Maridjan*
Rijswijk, The Netherlands

All of life tries to force you into boxes. You woke up this morning in a bed box, watched the news on a television box, took a shower in a box, left your house box to drive in your car box to go to your work box. Then you stare at a computer box or look at your cell phone box all day. Martijn does a great job in *Unboxed* of teaching you how to break free the your boxed-in mental limitations and experience life way beyond your current status! This is a great read for all church and marketplace leaders. I highly recommend it.

— *Dr. Keith Johnson*
"America's #1 Confidence Coach"
keithjohnson.tv
Spring Hill, Florida

In the day and time in which we live, we who call ourselves Christians cannot afford to be in a "box"! It's time to get unstuck and bust down the walls. The wisdom Martijn offers here will certainly give guidance and encouragement on how to do so! There is much to do. We can no longer afford to stay in the box!

— *Jack Henry*
Family Pastor
Tabernacle Baptist Church
Hiram, Georgia

Martijn is real and has a heart to help others succeed. *Unboxed* comes from a heart that is burning to see the church of Jesus Christ succeed and break through so we can impact the world with far more efficiency. Most people find change scary, but Martijn will help you realize God has amazing dreams about all of us and wants us to step into greater fruitfulness. If that is what you want, then read this book from a guy who has true burden from the Lord for His body.

—*David Sorensen*
Apostle, Godisreal.today
Poncha Springs, Colorado

Everyone has their own idea of what life and ministry looks like. It's based on our prior experiences or what someone has told us to be true. It's our box. It's safe, and it makes sense to us. But what happens when we step out of our box? That is when the real adventure begins. Martijn takes you on a journey that will shift your paradigm and help you become unboxed. If you want to move into the next level of your life and ministry, then get Martijn's book today. You will step out of your box and into your destiny.

— *Craig Johnson*
Senior Director of Ministries, Lakewood Church
Houston, Texas

There is great hope for our dreams again! Martijn expounds upon and delivers powerful steps for unlocking revelation that will thrust you into your true identity and purpose.

— *Marco Berlis*
Apostle
Oranjestad, Aruba

Martijn has a unique ability to interpret the Bible and make applications to life today, allowing his faith and courage to explore outside the box. *Unboxed* allowed me to relive and bring alive my experiences in Jerusalem. A must-read.

— *Bart Teal*
President, Blue Ribbon Schools of Excellence Inc.
Chapin, South Carolina

This book challenges me to discover how to critically think through what I'm doing in order to give God my best. It shows me the steps to take—and it came at just the right time as I evaluate kids ministry in our church. These principles will work in the secular world as well. I highly recommend *Unboxed*!

— *Karen Simmang*
Children's Pastor
Valley Ranch Baptist Church
Coppell, Texas

What if there was a reality far greater than your current experiences? What if God has something in store for you that you can't see from where you currently are? What if we have mindsets that keep us from seeing and entering a realm of greatness? In *Unboxed*, Martijn van Tilborgh takes you on a journey that will disrupt your current paradigm as he removes the veil and lets you peek into a future of hope, purpose, and abundance that God has in store for you. Buckle up—this is going to be quite a ride!

— *Dr. Joshua Fowler*
Author, Daily Decrees
LegacyLife.org
Dallas, Texas

Unboxed is an important book about a subject close to my heart. Change is necessary. We all say we want it, but do we really? We want the end result of change, but we avoid the process—which, of course, keeps us in our perfect little box. Martijn helps us to see why we should break out. I believe we are in a prophetically appointed time when we should no longer be satisfied with our status quo. You need a goal that is bigger than the box you are in. You were created by a big God who has big plans for you. *Unboxed* will help you make the steps to be constrained no more. Well done, Martijn!

> — *Rolph Hendriks*
> *Pastor, Power City*
> *Leiderdorp, The Netherlands*

Martijn takes you on a mental journey that opens up the palate of your mind and spirit to rethink and relearn what is possible. Many people today have fallen into the mode of "creative illiteracy." As American writer and futurist Alvin Toffler once stated: "The illiterate of the 21st century will not be those who cannot read and write, but those who cannot learn, unlearn, and relearn." *Unboxed* challenges you with the necessity of taking on the possibilities of relearning the notion that anything is possible. I highly recommend this book to anyone who knows that there is more to life than what they are currently experiencing.

— *Andrew Momon Jr.*
CEO, Momon Leadership Inc.
Servant Leadership and Lifestyle Expert
Atlanta, Georgia

Unboxed is an inspiring read for believers desiring a more passionate and purposeful life. Martijn invites us to exchange the often self-imposed boxes of limitations, assumptions, and even comfort for a life beyond our wildest dreams. *Unboxed* is a game-changing, paradigm-shifting read that expands your thinking so you can take courageous action and live more fulfilled.

— *Dr. Don Brawley III*
Pastor, Canaan Church
President, Influencers Global Leadership Company
Atlanta, Georgia

This book excites me and challenges me to leave the small, known boxes and step into God's unlimited that is always bigger, larger, and wider than one could ever imagine. Martijn has walked this journey himself and experienced the fruit of a life unboxed. God is looking for pioneers who will not settle for existing boxes or platforms but will go where no one else has gone before. *Unboxed* is that paradigm shift. This book is an unsettling challenge to go to new horizons that are beyond the limitations of your boxes.

— Shane Cooke
President and Founder, Shane Cooke Ministries
Melbourne, Australia

Unboxed is a must-read for Christians who are, or who are aspiring to become, biblical entrepreneurs. Martijn provides fresh keys to ultimate success and fulfillment in life, both personally and professionally.

— Mark J. Goldstein
President, Central Florida Christian Chamber
of Commerce
Orlando, Florida

In this book, my friend Martijn transparently shares his own experience of "unboxing"—the sometimes painful, often exhilarating process whereby God takes us from the comfortable environment we've built for ourselves and leads us into a new dimension of trusting Him. In the process, we discover that His plans are a lot riskier than we thought, but also that He's a lot more awesome than we imagined, proving Himself to be faithful in the midst of what can look a lot like chaos. Drawing on biblical insight and his own personal story, Martijn will challenge you to climb out of the familiar religious box you've made for yourself and step into the unknown of what God has for you.

— Matt Green
Vice President of Marketing, Pioneers-USA
former Editor, Ministry Today *magazine*
Orlando, Florida

This book changed my thinking. It makes sense that our loving and infinity creative God would design a gifting and calling for each one of us that is as individual as a fingerprint. What a joy to discover that my uniqueness is a gift, not an anomaly. Find your own color in God's infinite rainbow, and shine!

— John C. Morgan
world-renowned George W. Bush Impersonator
Motivational Speaker and Entertainer
Orlando, Florida

In every one of us lies God-given purpose and, most often, untapped potential. In *Unboxed*, Martijn initiates the conversation of "change"—the slow and sometimes difficult journey to first destroying the lies so that truth has ground to stand upon. Sit back, relax, and enjoy the ride!

— *Rebecca Faith*
Dramatic Communicator
Chattanooga, Tennessee

If you enjoy being challenged and value being inspired, *Unboxed* is the book for you! Martijn shares creative, applicable, and humorous real-life experiences to convey truth that many of us never even think to consider. *Unboxed* doesn't set out to simply expand your capacity; but it demands that your capacity and vision go into overdrive! The church desperately needs more writings like this to awaken it from slumber and challenge it to come alive in the world of the unboxed God!

— *Dr. Matthew Hester*
Greenville, South Carolina

Everyone has a spiritual gift, and everyone's gift is necessary. No one is left out. Everyone has a purpose. Everyone is included, and every one of us is needed. To not use your spiritual gift would be like not opening the birthday or Christmas gift that has your name on it. The packages sit unopened, looking beautiful, but the opportunity to use and enjoy what's in them is totally missed. Don't be like that unboxed gift! Don't miss your opportunity. Martijn's *Unboxed* will show you step-by-step how to be the gift God desires you to be for the sake of others.

— *Sam Hinn*
Pastor, The Gathering Place
Sanford, Florida

Unboxed: Uncovering New Paradigms
copyright ©2020 Martijn van Tilborgh

ISBN: 978-1-950718-49-8

Printed in the United States of America

cover design by Joe Deleon

Avail
225 W. Seminole Blvd., Suite 105
Sanford, FL 32771

UnBoxed

UncoveringNewParadigms

Martijn
van Tilborgh

Contents

Introduction 29

chapter 1
The Advantage Factor.............................. 39

chapter 2
Someone Is Waiting for You 51

chapter 3
A Mexican Blanket and a Bottle of Cheap Booze ...59

chapter 4
How to Become the Best Mediocre You 71

chapter 5
Getting Unboxed: Step by Step............................ 81

chapter 6
Think Bigger 93

chapter 7
Get Out! 109

chapter 8
Destroy the Box..125

chapter 9
Create 153

chapter 10
Boxes Kill Dreams.. 175

Additional Words from the Author........................189

Introduction

O K, I HAVE TO ADMIT … the first time it happened I felt a little weirded out. I remember very clearly picking up a call one day from an unrecognized number. After I said "Hello," there were a few seconds of what I can only describe as deafening silence. Suddenly I heard a strange sound that gave me goose bumps. It reminded me of a cruise ship leaving the port, sounding its horn. Later I came to find out the sound I heard so clearly was that of a shofar.

For those who do not know, a shofar is a wind instrument made from a ram's horn. Shofars were used throughout the Old Testament by the Jewish people to announce holidays, the Year of Jubilee, and a number of other events. Biblically, the shofar also represents the shout of God's victory or a prophetic declaration coming from the Lord Himself.

Like I mentioned, the whole thing initially was kind of an odd experience. But after a few of these encounters (yes, there were more), I pretty much got used to them.

In fact, I started to expect these calls because they were coming from a friend.

The person on the other end of the line was none other than 80-year-old Rosemarie von Trapp. Some of you may recognize that last name—and if you do, then yes, you are right. I'm talking about *that* family. Rosemarie is the daughter of Capt. Georg von Trapp, whose family story was told in *The Sound of Music*. No, she isn't the daughter of the actor Christopher Plummer who played Georg! I mean the *real* Capt. von Trapp.

Rosemarie and several other von Trapp family members had become frequent visitors in our meetings and engaged partners of our ministry. I had been in Vermont seven times where the von Trapps have a prestigious family lodge in the mountains. On one of our trips we held a leadership summit in their lodge. Leaders from all over the state had come together to attend this event.

It had been quite a ride, really, leading up to those days.

Only two years had passed since I and my family of five had set foot in the United States. Before that, we were full-time missionaries in South Africa, where we had lived for almost three years. At that time, I was convinced that we would probably live in Africa for the rest of our lives. Since God had called us there, I assumed He wouldn't change His mind.

We had moved to South Africa from the Netherlands, where I grew up. We had filled a storage container with all our possessions and shipped it to Cape Town, where we would be establishing our new lives. We moved into a house in there, got ourselves three dogs, put the kids in school, planted several churches, and focused on numerous social projects.

When God speaks, a single word from His mouth can change everything!

Little did we know that God had another plan for us.

When God speaks, a single word from His mouth can change everything! And that is exactly what happened. One Friday morning, one word from Him disrupted our entire lives. It changed everything, forever, in a moment's time. Both my wife, Amy, and I came to the sobering realization that (surprisingly) a new assignment had been given to us.

A mere three days later we arrived in the United States with only a few suitcases. I remember the mixed emotions I was having. A fear of the unknown and the adrenaline of God doing something exciting and new in our lives were both running through me. I had no idea what the heck I was supposed to do in America! Moving from one continent to another in a moment's time, based on a prompting of the Holy Spirit, may sound adventurous and cool; but the truth is, I was scared to death.

Back in South Africa, life was fairly easy. I was part of a ministry team that supported one another. We had our routines, projects, meetings and services that we focused on throughout each week. Honestly, looking back, I realize I had created a false sense of religious accomplishment by going through the motions.

Now, suddenly, I found myself overnight (literally) on the other side of the ocean where nobody had facilitated a ministry environment for me to be part of. There were no meetings, no projects, no routines to depend on. In other words, if I was not going to give birth to something authentic in the U.S., nothing was going to happen. At all.

Gone was the false sense of religious accomplishment. In its place was a true sense of desperation! I found myself praying desperately for God to show me the way! The funny thing about desperation is that it drives you to pay more attention to what God might be saying. The vacuum created by our trans-Atlantic move had now driven me to truly seek His face.

It is one thing to *feel* God calling you for something great. It's another thing to *experience it* firsthand.

This dramatic change in our lives propelled us into two full years of ministry that went beyond what we could ever have prayed for or imagined. The word "amazing" doesn't come close to describing what happened during those two years. The open doors, the connections, the opportunities, the experiences we had during that time were truly unprecedented for us.

It is one thing to *feel* God calling you for something great. It's another thing to *experience it* firsthand. I had personally heard God (before this time) telling me that I would travel the nations of the earth. That I would go throughout the world and preach. That He would open doors that had been closed. But—suddenly—I was living it! The time had arrived. This was it—I was there. I was in a place of purpose and destiny. I was moving from church to church to minister and preach. I jumped on planes multiple times a month to go from state to state, from nation to nation.

Many times I didn't even know where I was going until the Lord prompted me to go. All I knew was that I was to go to certain places—without having any idea what I would do in those places. And every time that happened, He came through. I was experiencing things you read about in books. Except this time, it was me in the story!

Many times I didn't even know where I was going until the Lord prompted me to go.

How could life get any better than this? I would wonder. *This is why we came to the United States. This is what I have wanted to give my life for. Doing the work of the ministry, impacting lives, and knowing that I am doing what I am supposed to do.*

I was living a life of purpose.

The friendship we developed with Rosemarie was the icing on the cake of our amazing ministry adventure. Her authentic and childlike faith was inspiring. Being introduced and connected to so many wonderful people along the way was an incredible experience. Many of those relationships still exist today.

Life was filled with purpose, with a sense of destiny being accomplished, with the joy and power of Spirit-led ministry. Like I said, to call it *amazing* didn't even describe it. Therefore, I had no idea back then that *all of that too had to stop.*

I was oblivious to the fact that God had an even bigger and different plan for us.

Looking back, though, it all makes perfect sense now. Seeing it in hindsight, I realize that what I was experiencing was only a fraction of what God had in store. I was like a kid playing in the shallow end of the pool, unaware of the adventures he would have when he realized there was a deep end waiting for him.

The truth was, that there was *so much more* that God had in store. I just couldn't see it. The limited paradigm I had about life and ministry had deceived me into thinking that what I was experiencing was about as good as it gets. Yet that paradigm was about to shift to something much bigger.

I didn't realize, really, that I had put myself in a box.

And it was a box that looked so big from the inside. But from God's viewpoint, it was too small. In context of what I am able to see today, I realize how insignificant that box really was—in light of what God had, and still has, in store for me. I needed some sort of intervention to show me a bigger world.

We all need an unboxing experience if we are truly going to experience the fullness of what God has in store for us.

I needed to be *unboxed*!

This book is the story of that unboxing process. It describes the journey I personally went through to become unboxed. But this book is about you, too; because the truth is, we all are in boxes. We all need an unboxing experience if we are truly going to experience the fullness of what God has in store for us. Chances are, you're just like I was—there is so much more beyond your current reality that you haven't even started to tap into.

Becoming unboxed, however, requires a journey that is not for the faint of heart. It takes courage and sacrifice to complete it. It will cost you everything, really.

However, along the way you will start to truly understand what drove the merchant in Matthew 13:45-46 to sell *everything* he owned to obtain the "pearl of great price" that Jesus described in His parable.

Again, the kingdom of heaven is like a merchant seeking beautiful pearls, who, when he had found one pearl of great price, went and sold all that he had and bought it.

This pearl can only be found outside the constraints of the box you are in. To find it, you will be required to leave the place where you are today. To obtain it, you will have to pay a price—a huge price! But I promise you, it will be well worth it. The reward is going to be incredible.

Are you with me? If your answer is yes, then follow me. And get ready to be unboxed!

chapter 1

The Advantage Factor

THE KINGDOM OF GOD IS BIG. Very big. In fact, it is so big that seeing only a glimpse of it will disrupt (and likely destroy) any box we have built for ourselves.

I got one of those glimpses on the night of Easter 2008, the night that changed my life forever and put me on the journey that helped me get unboxed.

I was confused, frustrated and, to be honest, I was annoyed with God. I sort of understood what Jonah was feeling after God grew a plant to provide him shade from the sun—just so He could send a worm to damage the plant and make it wither away (Jonah 4:6-8).

I was lying in bed that night asking myself questions: *Why would God do this to me? Why would He be so cruel and why does He have to be such a bully?*

I just didn't understand. The ministry I thought I had was gone. It had come quickly, but it seemed to have disappeared even quicker. Three unexpected things had happened.

- First, the financial crisis of 2008 had hit—and hit hard! During one of my ministry adventures, I had a divine appointment with someone who helped fund my ministry and connected me with an organization based in Iceland that supported me financially. Iceland essentially went bankrupt overnight. Their currency plummeted in a downward spiral to the point where it was worth only a fraction of its original value. This instantly dried up my financial resources, as the monthly support that I got from Iceland ceased.

- Second, the ministry I was part of at the time went through some hard stuff. We had been highly committed to this ministry for more than a decade; we had moved from continent to continent five times in our commitment to its vision. I don't regret any of it for even one second. However, a series of events led to a crisis in the ministry that caused it to implode. It shrunk to just a handful of people.

- Third, for some reason, certain doors that had been wide open suddenly closed. Instantly. In one instance, a leader with the network I had developed in Vermont created confusion about me among the statewide leaders, which resulted in resistance against my coming back there to minister. I was essentially shut out of the state by the same church leadership who had welcomed me with open arms just a year earlier.

Our financial situation had become bad. Really bad! It had happened so fast that I hadn't even been aware of the seriousness of the situation. I had added up all our debt and come to the realization that we owed well over $60,000 to various banks and institutions.

I felt like I was on the verge of a breakdown. We had just moved into a new apartment and had no clue how to pay our rent—in addition to all the other bills that had started to pile up quickly.

Now What ... ? (How About New Vision)

I remember looking at Amy in despair and asking her: "Now what?"

As soon as I spoke these two simple words something supernatural happened. Now, before I explain what happened next, I want you to understand one thing about me. I'm a pretty down-to-earth guy. I have known other people who have supernatural experiences like this all the time. Not me. In fact, I can probably count them on one hand.

I have known other people who have supernatural experiences like this all the time. Not me.

When I uttered the words, "Now what?" I was caught up in another realm in an instant. I'm not even sure how long I was there, as I had lost all sense of time. When I was "out there" I was struck with what I can explain only as "muteness." I couldn't speak. I could identify with what Zacharias must have experienced when the angel took away his speech (Luke 1:20).

I started crying, which I really don't do very often. My wife thought I was having a stroke and started to panic.

At that very moment I saw a story unfold in my spirit. It was the story of Jesus and His disciples. For three years they had the time of their lives—I saw it right in front of me. It was almost tangibly visible. It made me wonder, *How could life get any better than this for these disciples?*

They were walking with Jesus and got to learn from Him up close and personal. They were healing the sick. They were raising the dead. They were casting out demons. Every day they got to experience the amazing teaching that Jesus was giving to large crowds. They witnessed miracles where multitudes were fed supernaturally and where storms were calmed by the sound of His voice.

Wow! That was it—that was purpose. They were experiencing destiny like they never had before, like they never had even dreamed of before. They had reached the ultimate goal and purpose for their lives.

At least that's what they thought.

Then suddenly one day, their paradigm was disrupted when Jesus sat them down and spoke the following words: "*But very truly I tell you, it is for your good that I am going away*" (John 16:7a).

In other words, He told them that the amazing things they were experiencing were going to stop—had to stop. In fact, it would be to their advantage if all of it *did* stop.

In that moment, Jesus introduced them to a reality much bigger than the limited box they had created for themselves. The paradigm they lived in was about to be crushed in order to show them an advantage they couldn't see from where they were at that time. Sure, life was about as good as it gets in their paradigm. But from where God was sitting, there was more. Much, much more!

Their initial reaction was to quickly forget what they just heard Jesus tell them. They didn't want their current experience to stop. They loved it too much. Besides, what could be better than what they were experiencing? They were living life to the fullest (they thought).

Then, suddenly, it happened again—when they were least expecting it, the "impossible" happened. Jesus actually went away like He had said He would. What's more, one of their own even betrayed Him. In a moment's time they found themselves not in the middle of one of Jesus' incredible ministry adventures but, rather, gathered around a dead body in a tomb where Jesus had been laid to rest.

It's funny how our human minds work. We always tend to default back to what we know, based on our past experiences or the way we were raised or the things we were taught and the culture we grew up in. And that's exactly what the

disciples did. They went back to the only thing they knew
was "right."

We always tend to default back to what
we know, based on our past experiences
or the way we were raised or the things
we were taught and the culture we grew
up in.

They had grown accustomed to the excitement of Jesus'
ministry. All they knew how to do was to be around Him. So
when He died, the first thing they did was to have "church"
around a dead body. They gathered at the gravesite with
myrrh, linen, and perfume. What else could they do? They
defaulted back to what they knew, which was to be around
Him, wherever He was. And even though He was dead, at
least they made Him smell good with all the treatments
they were giving Him.

I suppose it gave them a false sense of religious
accomplishment.

Then after three days, even that illusion was taken from
them. At least within their paradigm it was. They still were

failing to see the advantage factor that Jesus had talked with them about! The truth was, Jesus was fully alive and well. Yet they couldn't see that from where they were sitting. He was just outside their current reality, where He was trying to get their attention so He could pull them outside of the box they had built for themselves.

As I was watching this story in the trancelike state I was in, something remarkable happened. It was as if my own life story was laid on top of this scenario I was watching unfold right in front of me. I experienced what the disciples must have experienced as they went through their crisis.

You can't be resurrected unless you die first. It's pretty simple, really!

I realized I was experiencing the things I was going through because of an advantage the Lord wanted to show me outside of the box I was in. As soon as I was able to peek beyond that box into a reality I didn't know even existed, I heard the sound of His voice saying:

"Everything must die first!"

I can still hear those words today as clearly as I heard them yesterday. In that moment I came to the realization that if we truly want to experience the fullness of His resurrection power, we will need to experience death first. You can't be resurrected unless you die first. It's pretty simple, really!

In an instant I was back to "normal" and able to explain to Amy what I had just experienced. I knew what I needed to do next. The following day I literally "killed" my ministry (or what was left of it), despite people in my life discouraging me to do so. I knew it had to be done.

My unboxing had now officially started.

Coaching Questions

1. In this chapter I share my story of frustration and confusion, which I thought was the result of the enemy trying to destroy me. Through my struggle I came to the conclusion that my frustration was only the result of the "box" that I had put myself in, and I started to discover the advantage factor He had in store for me. Are there any areas of frustration and confusion in your life that could possibly be the result of God trying to show you your "advantage"? What are they, and how is the Lord shifting your paradigm considering these struggles?

_____

_____

_____

_____

_____

_____

_____

_____

2. In this chapter I use the term "false sense of religious accomplishment" to describe the mental state of mind of the disciples as they gathered at the tomb around the dead body of Jesus. The glory of the past had gone, but they still defaulted back to what they had always done. They gathered and hung around Jesus! The power of the past had lifted and they failed to see the advantage factor for their lives.

_____

_____

_____

_____

_____

_____

3. As you evaluate your life and take an honest look at your ministry, do you feel that there are areas of busyness that give you a false sense of religious accomplishment? What are they and how do you feel you can change that?

_____

_____

_____

_____

_____

_____

_____

chapter 2

Someone Is Waiting for You

IN THE COURSE OF THIS BOOK I will break down the unboxing process into five steps, or phases, if you will. Breaking it down that way will help you travel the same journey I traveled in order to experience the abundant life that God has in store.

But before I do this, I first want to spend some time on the "why" behind this message.

In the book of John, we find the following scripture: *The thief comes only to steal and kill and destroy; I have come that they may have life, and have it to the full* (John 10:10).

We've all read this verse before. There are two things that I've learned from it.

1. You (and I) will face opposition. First, there is a force out there that wants to keep us from experiencing the fullness of God working in and through our lives. There is an enemy that seeks to steal, kill, and destroy the work of God in our lives. Someone is out to get us!

Many times "the thief" manifests himself in a very obvious way. He shows his true nature by literally attempting to bring destruction and death in our worlds that keep us from greatness.

The enemy even takes on a religious appearance in an attempt to keep us from greatness, while using the Word of God against us—to his advantage.

However, I have also discovered that he shows himself in another form that is far more deceiving and subtle. In fact, many times he comes camouflaged as an angel of light. He even takes on a religious appearance in an attempt to keep us from greatness, while using the Word of God against us—to his advantage.

One way he accomplishes that is by creating boxes. Religious boxes, that is. By creating boxes he can control and limit the experience we have as God's children. If he can make us believe the experience we can have with God is confined to the space we see within our box, then he can rob us of the abundance promised to us. He will even go as far as to deceive us into believing that our current experiences are the abundance God promised us.

These lies put us in a mental state wherein we simply believe that what we are experiencing in our current reality is, in fact, the abundant life Jesus promised us. He gets us to believe there is nothing more than our current reality. This is it!

I don't know about you, but when I look around, I have to be honest and say I am not happy with where we are as the church of Jesus Christ. If this is all there is, I have better things to do. I refuse to believe this is what His abundant life is. There must be more!

2. There is more—unbox it! This brings me to the second thing I learned from John 10:10, which is ... *there is more!*

Jesus has come so I may have life, and even life more abundantly! God has more for you than the life you have today. There is an abundance outside of your current paradigm that He wants you to tap into. What He has is more abundant than what we're experiencing today.

Now, some of you might be content with where you are in life. You may not have a desire to break out of your box. That is, of course, possible—your life may be easy and comfortable for you just the way it is. You have your job, your home, your car, your dog, your ministry, your family, and life is pretty great. Really, what more do you need? I get it. Sometimes it's just easier to keep things the way they are. Don't rock the boat. Everything is going well, and there is no need to disturb that.

If this is you, then what I'm about to share is very important for you to understand. Are you ready?

Here it is: *It's not all about you!*

Yes, that's right. You are not the center of the universe. Now, of course, you are important in God's eyes; don't get me wrong. But there is another side of that coin, which is—everyone else! The abundant life is not just for you; it is for everyone. A price was paid for you, yes; but guess what?

There is a world full of people out there destined for that same abundance.

By staying in your box, you effectively show the world around you a wrong image of the God you pretend to represent.

By staying inside your tiny box, you not only settle for second (third or fourth) best in your own life, but you also keep others from experiencing what they are waiting for. Whether they realize it or not, they hunger for a manifestation of the fullness of God in their lives, not a manifestation of the religious box you are in. By staying in your box, you effectively show the world around you a wrong image of the God you pretend to represent.

Who's Waiting for You to Be Unboxed?

Here's what Paul says in the book of Romans: *"For the creation waits in eager expectation for the children of God to be revealed"* (Romans 8:19).

Whether or not creation knows it, creation is waiting for something. And the waiting continues to exist until something profound happens. When that happens, the waiting will stop.

The world around us is waiting for you and me to become who we are supposed to be.

Creation is waiting for the sons of God to be revealed in the earth. The world around us is waiting for you and me to become who we are supposed to be. Creation waits for a full manifestation of God in and through you so that His kingdom can become visible on earth the same way it is already manifest in heaven.

The only way for this to happen is for you and me to get out of our religious boxes we created. The only place where you can be revealed for who you were created to be is outside of your box. As long as we live within the limitations of the world we've created for ourselves, creation will wait.

We must be unboxed. Who is waiting for you to be unboxed? Someone is waiting for you!

Coaching Questions

1. In this chapter I talk about "the thief" who comes to steal and to destroy. I explain how sometimes the thief manifests himself in a very obvious way, but that sometimes he comes in a way that is far more deceptive and subtle by making you believe that the life you are living is in fact the abundance of God. As you read through this chapter did the Lord show you any areas to which this type of "stealing" applies? How do you feel the thief has robbed you?

_____

_____

_____

_____

_____

_____

_____

2. Romans 8 teaches us that creation waits for the revealing of the sons of God. Do you feel like you are already

walking in that purpose in your life? Do you feel that God is revealing Himself through you effectively as you fulfill your prophetic purpose? On what evidence do you base your answer?

_____

_____

_____

_____

_____

_____

_____

_____

chapter 3

A Mexican Blanket and a Bottle of Cheap Booze

I F YOU DESIRE TO HAVE a high-impact ministry and an abundant life beyond your current reality, then you are going to need to embrace one thing: *change!*

Without change, things stay the same, results remain mediocre, and our lives become stagnant. Almost everyone likes the idea of change, yet embracing change is a different story. We do the things we do because we've been taught those things from a young age. Our behavior is rooted in how we've been raised; the culture in which we were brought up contributed to behavioral patterns. In turn, those patterns led us to create limitations and boxes for ourselves over the years.

The creative power of God Himself lives on the inside of each and every one of us.

We view the world around us through a paradigm established by these collective factors, which have created a limitation, an invisible barrier, or a ceiling that keeps us small.

Yet we were created for something else: *greatness!*

The creative power of God Himself lives on the inside of each and every one of us. It has the potential to infuse us with divine inspiration and a vision born from His heart. Yet so much of what we do is the result of a paradigm that limits us to mediocre results—at best.

Albert Einstein said this: "We cannot solve our problems with the same thinking we used when we created them."

Those are profound words. We tend to look for solutions to problems within the context of our current paradigms. Problems that wouldn't even be problems if it wasn't for the paradigm we are in. Sometimes our boxes create problems that actually would be irrelevant outside the parameters of that box. Removing the box completely would solve the problem completely and instantly.

I know, I know! This sounds complex. Let me attempt to explain it with a story about something I experienced a few years back.

There's No Such Thing as a Free Breakfast

A pastor from a local church invited me for a free breakfast at his church.

"A free breakfast?" I asked?

"Yes!" he said. "A free breakfast! Bring your wife and we'll have fun. There are a ton of other people coming. You'll enjoy yourself."

Of course, I knew that there is no such thing as a free breakfast. Sometime, someone is going to pay for it. I somehow had this uncomfortable feeling that even though this was an opportunity that was presented as "free," we would be the ones paying for this breakfast.

I was right!

Looking back, the best way to explain the whole experience is by calling it a "Christian timeshare presentation." Have you ever sat through one of these? I love them because of my interest in sales, marketing, and communication. I love to analyze the psychology behind these tours and pre-sentations. If you've ever been in the Caribbean countries, you've probably had someone try to lure you into one of these presentations.

I remember being in Cozumel, Mexico, for a day, when I was convinced to go into one. I was bribed with a Mexican blanket and a bottle of some sort of cheap, local alcoholic drink. As a result, I ended up listening to a two-hour story on how I should own property in Cozumel. The pitch was very compelling, I remember. Even to the point that I actually considered spending tens of thousands of dollars on a timeshare ownership in Mexico. It all made sense. If it hadn't been for the fact that I didn't have money at the time, I probably would have done it.

The free breakfast at the church ended up being a very similar experience. It didn't take long for me to figure out what it was really all about. This was about the church wanting to expand into a bigger, better, nicer facility. The breakfast was a platform for pitching the new building project the pastor wanted to initiate.

I have to say, the sales pitch was convincing. Everything he said sounded logical and made perfect sense. Even the breakfast was actually pretty tasty, which put us all in a good mood. It wasn't long before the first people in the room to donate started reaching for their checkbooks. It was like a QVC presentation. The lines were now open!

Boxed-In Thinking in Action

Yet, while listening to the pastor and his seemingly flawless pitch, I couldn't help but notice that something wasn't sitting well with me. I just couldn't put my finger on it. Besides the fact that I think new building projects for churches are very boring, predictable, and expected (everybody wants a bigger, better building), I knew on a deeper level that something was wrong. Not that there is something wrong with a better building, necessarily, but they sure can become a ball and chain down the road (on multiple levels) if you're not careful.

Then suddenly I had an instant epiphany. I knew what was wrong!

It was the paradigm (or box) in which the sales pitch was delivered. You see, we structure our ministries according to certain assumptions. I'll share more about this later in the book. But, for now, what I mean by that statement is rooted in what I mentioned before—that certain problems will not even be problems if the box is removed.

I remember one of the arguments the pastor used to support his pitch for the new building. He said this:

"Well my friends, we all know that on Sunday morning we have experienced some amazing growth. We are super thankful to the Lord for this amazing blessing on our ministry. As you have noticed, this building we are in has become a little tight. One example is this room next door. It comfortably holds 40 children during a Sunday morning service. For the last several weeks we've been having 50 children in that room. It has become too tight. If we want to have a bigger capacity to minister to more kids, we need to have a bigger facility. I propose to you this new building plan. Look at the blueprint I'm showing you here. It's going to require $2.6 million to get started on this project. I want to ask you to seek the Lord to find out what you should give."

Now, on the surface that all sounds great right? What's wrong with his pitch? You can't argue with him for wanting to minister to more children. I can certainly appreciate his desire to take the ministry to the next level.

Here's what's wrong with the picture he painted: the box, and the paradigm in which his pitch was communicated. The box controlled his message to the point that it was reduced to something that could happen only within a religious, predefined set of rules.

Think about it!

By saying, "We need a bigger building in order to minister to more kids," he was assuming something that was critically wrong. He was assuming that the only way they could minister to kids was in that room next door! That's essentially like telling God that He is limited to the invisible parameters of a box—in this case, the literal box of a limited-space room in the church!

Unboxed Thinking: A Better Way

I'm sure he wasn't the only one in the church who saw it that way. In fact, let's insert ourselves into this conversation and imagine we think the same way. Somewhere along the way, then, our mind-set has become: "We have decided that children's ministry takes place within these set of rules. We need a building, a children's pastor/leader, a curriculum, and so on, in order to impact that generation in our community."

Where do these assumptions come from?

Somewhere, we've been robbed by the thief who, Jesus said, comes to steal. He robs, not in an obvious way, but in a very subtle way. He made us believe that somehow it's acceptable to spend $2.6 million on something that creates … what?

Marginal change!

Let's say we did spend all that money on the new building. The limitation of 40 kids is gone; but now it's replaced by another limitation of, let's say, 100 kids. There is no businessperson in the world who would invest that kind of money for such a small return. He or she would think, *There has to be a better way.*

And they'd be right!

What would happen if we were somehow able to remove all the assumptions from our thinking and allow our spirits to be in tune with God's Spirit?

So, then, what would happen if we were able to remove that box? What would happen if we were somehow able to remove all the assumptions from our thinking and allow our spirits to be in tune with God's Spirit to get new, innovative, creative ideas from Him on how to do ministry outside of our current view of what is possible?

Think about this. What if we were to take a fraction of that $2.6 million and facilitate a platform from which we could equip the church families to minister to kids? Not so much by telling them how to minister, but by allowing them to tap into the creative inspiration of the Spirit in order to devise forms of ministry that suit the individual. Not ministry that's done in church on Sunday morning, but ministry done in the community as part of people's everyday life.

The families in our churches are already in contact with the families in the community. Everyone's kids already go to the same sports clubs, schools, birthday parties, and other activities.

If we were able to facilitate a platform that would equip people to become effective in the sphere where they already are planted, wouldn't that be more effective than building a bigger building—as well as cheaper, and more fulfilling, exciting, and diverse?

You see, too many times we tell people how the giant *should be* defeated. We tell them to put on Saul's armor and go forth bearing his heavy sword because "that's the way" this battle is fought. That's the way the giant is defeated. But what would happen if we instead allowed people to find "their sling" (whatever that means for them) and face the giant in *their* faith instead of ours? Then how many giants do you think you would slay? And on a shoestring budget! What is the cap on the number of children you can impact within *that* paradigm?

That's right! *There is no limit!*

Coaching Questions

1. As you read through this chapter, what were some of your assumptions that were challenged?

_____

_____

_____

_____

_____

_____

_____

2. How was your mindset expanded as a result of the challenge that you experienced?

_____

_____

_____

_____

_____

_____

_____

3. What do you see now, that you didn't see before?

_____

_____

_____

_____

_____

_____

_____

_____

chapter 4

How to Become the Best Mediocre You

WHEN YOU ALIGN YOUR MIND with a fixed paradigm (or box), something very interesting happens. The limited belief system you created for yourself starts to limit your actions. This then creates an environment that becomes the breeding ground for something completely foreign to the nature of God.

It is called *competition*.

"Competition" is not a word that appears in God's dictionary. It is something that never was part of His original design for creation. Competition is something we created. Not as much because we invented it as much as our tendency to create religious boxes resulted in an environment in which competition lives.

Mediocre vs. Great

Throughout the entire New Testament, there is a theme among the disciples that seems to re-occur quite a bit. They talk about it a lot. They appear very concerned with the question of who is the greatest among them.

Of all things the disciples could have been concerned about, the question that seemed to occupy each of them the most was whether or not he was greater than the next disciple.

"*At that time the disciples came to Jesus, saying, 'Who, then, is greatest in the kingdom of heaven?'*" (Matthew 18:1, NIV). This is just one reference that mentions the ongoing conversation on the same topic.

Isn't that interesting? Of all things they could have been concerned about, the question that seemed to occupy each of them the most was whether or not he was greater than the next disciple. We tend to read these stories and shake our heads, not realizing that the very boxes we've created in our lives and ministries facilitate that same narrative.

I'll illustrate this by sharing a scripture with you about John the Baptist.

"For I say to you, among those born of women there is not a greater prophet than John the Baptist; but he who is least in the kingdom of God is greater than he" (Luke 7:28, NIV).

This verse is fascinating to me. It speaks about two paradigms:

1. Those born of women
2. Those who are in the kingdom of God

Whenever Jesus compares and contrasts these two "worlds" and shows us the difference between them, I like to believe that He wants us to learn something.

In His first example, Jesus speaks about a world or system in which there can be only one who is the greatest. There can be only one winner in this "system." The climate and culture in this environment is one of competition. Everyone is competing for that No. 1 spot. In this example, Jesus had already given that spot to someone called John the Baptist. John was the greatest within that category. Nobody could take his spot. It belonged to John!

Imagine being in an environment like that. That really sucks, right? You put effort and hard work into it, all the while knowing you can never become the greatest because that spot has already been taken. You're going to have to settle for second place … at best. How discouraging!

We find the greatest one and model our ministries accordingly and strive to be as much like No. 1 as we can be.

In this world, John becomes the role model for greatness. Everyone in that world strives to become like John, yet they know they will never match up to his greatness. Everyone in that "box" knows they will always be inferior to the one who has already been proclaimed the greatest.

In our ministries we do exactly the same thing the disciples did. We find the greatest one and model our ministries accordingly and strive to be as much like No. 1 as we can be.

These days that No. 1 spot is taken by a man named Joel …
Joel Osteen, that is. You may have heard of him.

We look at Joel and make him and his ministry model
the ultimate goal. We think, *If I can do only half as well as
Joel, then I'm doing great.* This way of thinking is carnal.
We do ourselves (and God) injustice by thinking like this.
This mentality or paradigm creates hierarchy and ungodly
competition. It keeps us mediocre.

We focus on how we can earn more points on the scoreboard, not realizing the scoreboard we're looking at is ref-
erencing how we rank in a world of mediocrity. The best
thing that can happen to us within that "system" is that you
and I become the best mediocre versions of ourselves that
we can be.

Authentic by Design, Artificial by Choice

It's how you become the best mediocre you that you can
be. If that's the game you want to play, then you should
certainly keep doing what you are doing. Who knows,
maybe you can do a little better than that person next
door.

Personally, I would like to be part of the other world
Jesus talks about. That world is much, much bigger. In that

world, even the smallest person is bigger than the winner in the other box.

How does that work? Well it's simple. We have to remove the boxes in our lives!

A businessman once told me: "If you can't be No. 1 in your category, you need to create a new category for yourself to be No. 1 in." Those are some great words! They made me think about God's categories for us.

We all are endowed with gifts that have been given only to us and nobody else.

Ask yourself this question: How many categories do you think God has for His people? The answer is so simple, yet so hard for us to understand. His portfolio of categories for his children is endless. There is no end to his diversity in the plans and purposes He has for us.

By unique, authentic, divine design we all are created different. We all are endowed with gifts that have been given only to us and nobody else. Therefore, I need to play a role in the earth that only I can play. Only I can dominate my category because by definition nobody else fits my category. I am one-of-a-kind!

God's kingdom is a world that is created to facilitate extreme diversification. Instead of it being a hierarchy organized vertically, it is horizontally organized through diversification. It requires a different way of thinking. Once we grasp it and become who we are supposed to be in His image, we automatically trump the greatest in the inferior carnal world.

Isn't that amazing? I sure think so!

It's actually super logical and simple. Yet, at the same time, we tend to default back to modeling ourselves according to ministry templates delivered to us by "the greatest." As long as we try to model ourselves after categories that are dictated by others, we miss the mark. All you can do at that point is to attempt to become the best mediocre you that you can possibly be.

There's a New World Outside That Box

God wants to bring us into a new world. The world of the kingdom. In this world you'll find identity and purpose on an individual, unique level. The manifestation of it is something that has no point of reference in the world we live in. It cannot be compared with anything else that exists around us because it's unique by definition.

If we are going to be part of this world, then it is going to require a mental shift that will naturally break the box we've been in for so long. Things we always assumed were normal will no longer be normal. Your new mind-set will result in new behavioral patterns that, in turn, will disrupt your environment and the people around you. Remember what the Bible teaches us about new wine:

"And no one pours new wine into old wineskins. Otherwise, the new wine will burst the skins; the wine will run out and the wineskins will be ruined" (Luke 5:37, NIV).

New wine requires a new skin if it is going to be preserved. Those in the kingdom will have a new skin to pour the new wine in so that we can become great in our own authentic selves. That's where God wants to bring us. That's where the church becomes effective. That's where His kingdom will come on earth as it is in heaven.

That's where the sons of God are revealed so creation can stop waiting.

Coaching Questions

1. In this chapter I talk about two systems. One that breeds competition and one that breeds a creative expression of God's purpose through you. As you were reading through this chapter did you recognize the first system in areas of your own life in which you simply model your activity after a template that was handed to you? If so, what are the specifics?

_____

_____

_____

_____

_____

_____

_____

2. What can you do practically to position yourself within the context of that second system in which even the smallest is greater than the greatest of that first system?

_____

_____

_____

_____

_____

_____

_____

3. What decisions do you feel you need to make to get positioned to be propelled into the next level that God has in store for you?

_____

_____

_____

_____

_____

_____

_____

chapter 5

Getting Unboxed: Step by Step

OK, BASIC TRAINING HAS BEEN COMPLETED. I hope that you are now ready to start taking the journey. The unboxing process is about to begin. Are you ready?

In the next five chapters, I will start to break down the unboxing process step by step. I will systematically show you both the mental shifts we need to go through in each phase as well as scriptural references that reinforce and solidify each point. Each step will build on the previous step in a logical manner.

The prophet Isaiah put it this way:

"For precept must be upon precept, precept upon precept, line upon line, line upon line (Isa. 28:10, NJKV).

God is systematic. What He gives us tomorrow builds on what He gives us today. When you read through the Bible you'll see that same process throughout. What he did with Abraham built on what He did with Adam. What He did with Moses built on what He did with Abraham. Even what He does today builds on what He did in the book of Acts.

God is systematic. What He gives us tomorrow builds on what He gives us today.

The same is true for this process. It is crucial that we truly understand each of these steps and embrace them in order one at a time. If we don't, we start building a leaning tower. It will be just a matter of time before the tower falls.

So if you're ready, then let's get started.

Step 1: Awareness

It all starts with one thing: Awareness!

Without awareness we are clueless of our own situation. Remember my story? I didn't have a clue that what I was doing in ministry was limited by the box I created for myself. I didn't realize I was living in mediocrity compared to what God had in store. God had so much more in store for me, but I couldn't see beyond the paradigm that obstructed my view. I needed to be made *aware*, which happened through the supernatural experience I shared with you earlier.

All of us will need some divine intervention once in a while to show us a world beyond what we can see from where we are today.

In the book of Revelation we read the following:

"After this I looked, and there before me was a door standing open in heaven. And the voice I had first heard speaking to me like a trumpet said, 'Come up here, and I will show you what must take place after this'" (Revelation 4:1, NIV).

This scripture intrigues me. Here was John on the island of Patmos, and he had this vivid vision. He saw an open door in heaven. From where he was standing he could see that the door was open, but he couldn't see what was on the other side.

Maybe that is you. You know that there must be more to life than what you are currently experiencing. You know

God wants to break you of the same old mediocre environment that you are part of. You just don't know what or how to do it.

So often we find ourselves in the same position as John. God has an open door for us, but we can't see beyond that door because of our vantage point. We somehow need to shift in order to be able to see beyond it. On the other side of the open door there are things that must take place. Things pertaining to our future.

God has an open door for us, but we can't see beyond that door because of our vantage point.

Even though the door was open, John was unable to peek through that door in order to see what those things were. Unless he shifted to a higher place to establish a different vantage point he was going to be stuck where he was.

How Un-Awareness Gets in God's Way

We need a similar paradigm shift once in a while if we're going to be unboxed. We need an encounter with God who will help make us aware of our limited positioning.

Here's a great story that helped me tremendously over the years. It's the story about the man with the measuring line in his hand from the book of Zechariah:

Then I raised my eyes and looked, and behold, a man with a measuring line in his hand. So I said, "Where are you going?" And he said to me, "To measure Jerusalem, to see what is its width and what is its length." And there was the angel who talked with me, going out; and another angel was coming out to meet him, who said to him, "Run, speak to this young man, saying: 'Jerusalem shall be inhabited as towns without walls, because of the multitude of men and livestock in it. For I,' says the Lord, 'will be a wall of fire all around her, and I will be the glory in her midst" (Zechariah 2:2-5, NKJV).

On the surface this portion of scripture may not be more than a story, but on a deeper level it holds a tremendous revelation. Let's unpack this portion of scripture by paraphrasing the story verse by verse.

Here is a man with a measuring line in his hand, and he is on his way to measure Jerusalem. He is full of zeal. His heart is probably in the right place, and he loves the Lord. He's excited about the city of God, Jerusalem, and is committed to give his contribution to the building of that city.

His heart was in the right place. There seemed to be nothing wrong with this picture. It was just another day in the "office" for this man. He was happy to do the work of the Lord, building the city of God.

This man is like many of us. We're excited and committed to do the work of the ministry. We want to build the city of God. Our hearts are in the right place, and we can't wait to see that "city" completed so it can become a blessing to many.

Again, on the surface everything seemed fine. It's a great story. Yet on a deeper level there was a concern. An angel appears on the scene, and he actually abruptly stops the man from doing what he is doing. He says, in effect: "What do you think you're doing? Don't you know that Jerusalem shall be inhabited as towns without walls?"

The angel made the man aware of something very important that changed everything in relation to the activity the man was planning. The angel pointed out that Jerusalem, the city he was measuring and helping to build, wasn't going to have any walls.

Wow! That was a mental shift for this man. In fact, it was a game-changing revelation.

Everything he did and everything he was planning to do was based on the assumption that surely this city he was going to build was going to have walls. His whole ministry was founded on that assumption. He was planning to build a walled city. Yet, meanwhile, God had never intended Jerusalem to have any walls to begin with.

God had never intended Jerusalem to have any walls to begin with.

An awareness had come to the man by supernatural intervention that changed the game he was in forever. Remember, the primary tool this man had brought was a measuring line. He was specialized in using it. He was an expert at architecting blueprints for building walled cities. Now he comes to find out that the city he is trying to build is not going to have any walls whatsoever. The very thing he had become excellent in had become irrelevant in context of this new information he just received. He somehow had to unlearn the very thing he had studied all his life!

How do you measure a city without walls? How do you even plan to build a city without walls? Basically, you can't.

Yet, God wants a wall-less city anyway. God is making this man aware that what He is envisioning for the city is unmeasurable!

God says to him: "Hey! Don't you know? I cannot be measured, and neither can the city that I'm building."

He continues to explain to the man this city will have a multitude of people in it and that He Himself will be a wall of fire around them. In other words, wherever the people of God are, that's where the wall will be. Not because we build it for God, but because God Himself will be it.

Wow! That's amazing.

Why Standards Might Not Be What They Seem

Think about this question for a moment. What is a "measuring line"? Well, it's a measuring tool that references a standard that once was created by man. Not by God, but by man! Somebody at some point in history decided that a foot is a foot. Where I'm from, the Netherlands, we use the metric system. We use meters. The thing about meters is that at some point, someone (probably Mr. Meter) decided that a meter is a meter. He set the standard right then and there.

From that point onward, anything that ever had to be measured was measured by that standard. Every measuring line created since referenced that man's standard.

Could it be that we have measuring lines in our minds that reference a standard that was not meant to be a standard to begin with? Could it be that we are working on assumptions that we need to be made aware of? Could it be that God is trying to remove the measuring lines by which we measure our work?

In God's city, each person is supposed to give birth to a uniquely unexpected expression of who God is.

So many times we have strategic ministry meetings to plan how we will grow our ministries, and we set parameters for what this is going to look like. God says, "I cannot be measured." You cannot architect a wall-less city. In God's city, each person is supposed to give birth to a uniquely unexpected expression of who God is. It cannot be measured. It cannot be planned.

Like the man with the measuring line, we need to be made aware of this so we will cease putting effort in strengthening the box we're in. Instead, we become aware of the box—which is absolutely necessary before going to the next step.

Before we can be unboxed we must be made aware that we are in a box. Like the man with the measuring line, we might not be aware we are in a box.

In Step 1 of the process, God is telling us a story. He explains there is a box. And guess what? We are in it. Unless we start to see that, we will continue to build walled cities and keep Jerusalem from the multitudes who are destined to live in it.

Coaching Questions

1. This chapter starts the "unboxing" process with step 1, which is "awareness". Did God make you aware of anything that you couldn't see before in the process of reading this chapter? Please write down the details of that experience.

_____

_____

_____

_____

_____

_____

_____

2. In this chapter I explain how "measuring rods" in our mind keep us from building accurately what God wants us to build because of assumptions we have in our mind on how to build. What measuring rods have you identified in your thinking?

_____

_____

_____

_____

_____

_____

_____

_____

chapter 6

Think Bigger

WHEN I WAS NINETEEN, I lived in a communal home with eleven other guys my age. The church I was part of at the time had quite a few of these homes. It was an incredible time of spiritual growth, understanding the Word of God, and learning how to walk by faith. The house we lived in was on a typical Dutch canal in the center of a city called Utrecht. It was a pretty big house (by Dutch standards anyway), but since there were eleven of us, I still had to share my room with three other guys. It was very crammed, but I wouldn't have missed it for anything.

Incredible things happened during that season. We were a passionate bunch of radical young kids who sometimes would do very unconventional things to spread the gospel. We saw miracles of all sorts, people delivered from demons, and tons of people come to Christ. We were on the streets of the city almost daily, and almost everybody who lived in the city center knew about us or had attended one of our services.

News Flash: What If We're Wrong ... ?

One of the things I enjoyed most from that time were the late-night conversations with the other guys in the house. We would just hang out and share our hearts. Sometime we would talk about theological issues. Other times we would share stories of what the Lord was doing in and through our lives.

I remember one of those conversations very clearly. It is still with me as if it happened yesterday. Someone in the group posed the question:

"What if we're wrong?"

"What do you mean 'wrong?'" we asked.

"Well, so many people read the same Bible I'm reading, and they all seem to come to different conclusions of what the words on these pages mean," he said. "There are so many different interpretations. Obviously not everyone can be right!

"What if half of what we believe is the result of our own interpretation of the scripture and not God's interpretation?" he continued. "What if the majority of what we believe, we believe simply because we've been told by other people that it's true? But what if it isn't?"

Well, that was a good point. It was a scary thought, really. I noticed one of the guys who was part of the conversation had a nervous look on his face. God was speaking to him through this question: *What if we were all wrong?*

This guy in particular was known to be someone who would devour books. He would learn anything he could learn. He had shelves full of books on all kinds of spiritual topics. He had a lot of knowledge.

When the question was posed, his mind went to a place where he started to realize that being wrong was a true possibility. He wondered how much of what he had learned over the years was actually wrong information that kept him further from God's desired intent rather than closer? And how many hours of "work" did it represent that was wasted along the way? That thought was freaking him out.

Suddenly I had the solution to the problem. I presented it to the group.

"Why don't we pray and ask God to take away everything we know?" I asked. "Why don't we put all our knowledge on the altar and start from scratch? Why don't we ask Him to take 100 percent of what we know, even the things we are certain about, and ask Him to give back only what is truly His?"

Making an inventory of your belief system is one of the best things you can do if you want to get out of your little box.

It was so simple—yet so difficult. I remember the look on the face of my friend as he was trying to compute the balance of the cost of such a prayer.

"What if only 10 percent came back?" he asked. "Or worse, what if only 2 percent came back? That would be a disaster."

Obviously praying a prayer like that is the best thing you can do. What could be better than removing false information from your thinking? Sticking your head in the sand doesn't help anyone.

I'm sharing this story because making an inventory of your belief system is one of the best things you can do if you want to get out of your little box. In fact, it is a crucial step in getting out.

Step 2: Thinking Bigger

Step 2 in the process is all about thinking bigger. It's about thinking outside the box that you have become so accustomed to. This is extremely hard because it challenges someone to the core of their belief system and, therefore, their behavior.

How is that, you ask?

Well, if you are taught something and you choose to believe it, then that teaching will contribute to form a belief system. Ultimately your actions are going to align with that belief system. These actions will form a behavior pattern. Your behavior, in turn, is going to render results that directly correlate to the original thought you chose to believe at the beginning of this process.

Now let's back-engineer that quickly.

If you want different results in your life, you have to change your behavior. The only way to change your behavior is to change what you believe. And you can change what you believe only if you are challenged in what you know is right. It's called the reforming of the mind. If you want different results, you must change your mind! In order to change your mind, you have to challenge what you believe. There is no other way.

The Feast of Unleavened Bread

Here is a story for you from the book of Exodus:

For seven days you are to eat bread made without yeast. On the first day remove the yeast from your houses, for whoever eats anything with yeast in it from the first day through the seventh must be cut off from Israel (Exodus 12:15, NIV).

This passage talks about a feast God instructed the Israelites to celebrate when they were in Egypt. Before I go into the prophetic symbolism of what this means for us today, let's look at the back story.

At the time when Moses instructed the Israelites to celebrate the feast of unleavened bread, they had been in bondage for 430 years. Let that sink in for a little bit.

The Israelites had become the chosen people of God through His covenant with Abraham. But they originally had come to Egypt by divine intervention to escape starvation during a time of famine in what is now Israel—in what became the Promised Land. They had come as a family—God had sent Joseph ahead of his family to become a father to Pharaoh (Genesis 45:8) so he could facilitate a place for his family members to live during the famine. This plan was supposed to be temporary. Yet when they stayed too long in this God-ordained season, growing from a family into a nation, that season became a limitation to them. In fact, their extended stay in Egypt became a curse, which led to their being slaves for hundreds of years.

The Israelites' extended stay in Egypt became a curse, which led to their being slaves for hundreds of years.

Now, when I read a story like this, I always ask myself: What does this story mean for *me*? Remember, these were God's people. Not some Gentile nation. God's people! People who had a covenant with God Himself.

This story is about us! Apparently it is possible for God's people to be in a place of bondage. In fact, it appears to be possible not only to be in bondage, but also to be in bondage from generation to generation for hundreds of years.

Imagine growing up in an environment like that! You know who God is. You know where you came from. You know about God's covenant for you. You have all that information. Yet you are living a life that is completely foreign to the plan of God.

It is possible for God's people to work their butts off and toil day and night to build something that is completely foreign to God's intended purpose.

I can imagine after 430 years of that, you simply believe being in covenant with God looks like your personal experience. Again, these were God's people. This story is about us! You and me. But they weren't just enslaved in a foreign land where they were far removed from their true inheritance. There was something else.

Apparently it is possible for God's people to work their butts off and toil day and night to build something that is completely foreign to God's intended purpose. That's a scary thought, isn't it? Their 430 years of labor didn't simply produce something different from what God had envisioned—it literally fortified the enemy's empire!

Wow! Let that sink in for a moment.

This is more than a Sunday school story. Could it be that this story is about us? Could it be that a lot of our well-intended efforts we call "ministry" are in fact the building of pyramids? I think we should at least consider the possibility. And, by the way, pyramids may look awesome, but they're really just massive, elaborate tombs. There's nothing alive in them. They're literally "dead works."

What can we learn here? Well, let's read what happened in Exodus:

During that long period, the king of Egypt died. The Israelites groaned in their slavery and cried out, and their cry for help because of their slavery went up to God. God heard their groaning and he remembered his covenant with Abraham, with Isaac and with Jacob. So God looked on the Israelites and was concerned about them (Exodus 2:23-25, NIV).

It appears that at some point, Israel had had enough. I'm not sure why it took them 430 years to get there, but I guess the important part is that they did get there ultimately. They cried out. They'd simply had enough. "God, there must be more!" they said. "Take us out of this miserable place."

God heard their cry and acknowledged them. The escape plan was put in motion! When God chose the people, He went to look for a man who could lead them. He found Moses at the burning bush and sent him to deliver the people. The interesting thing here is that the escape plan was to celebrate the feast of unleavened bread. Moses called the elders together and gave them the instructions. Let's read it again:

> *For seven days you are to eat bread made without yeast. On the first day remove the yeast from your houses, for whoever eats anything with yeast in it from the first day through the seventh must be cut off from Israel* (Exodus 12:15, NIV).

Now, what does this mean to us prophetically? If you study "leaven" in the Bible, you will eventually come upon a New Testament verse in which Jesus talks about the "leaven of the Pharisees and Sadducees":

> *Then Jesus said to them, "Take heed and beware of the leaven of the Pharisees and the Sadducees"* (Matthew 16:6, NKJV).

In this verse, He's referring to the "corrupted doctrine" of the Pharisees and the Sadducees. Moses' instruction to the Israelites to remove the leaven from their houses for seven days prophetically speaks about the corrupted doctrine. As we've already seen, your doctrine or belief system determines your actions and behavior. By removing the "leaven" we remove wrong belief systems from our thinking. We allow our minds to think outside of the box that we have been in for so long.

What do we need to remove from our belief system that will bring us an escape for our limitation?

Food for Thought: What's Your Escape Plan?

For the Israelites, that box lasted for 430 years. How long has it been for us? What do we need to remove from our belief system that will bring us an escape for our limitation?

Note that the Israelites had to celebrate the feast of unleavened bread for seven days. *Seven* speaks about "fullness." Before they could come into unity and celebrate the

Passover lamb, they had to come together and systematically remove the leaven, until the process had come to its fullness. Then, and only then, were they able to escape their limitation.

Note also that after they left Egypt, God instructed them to celebrate the same feast every year. They had to repeat the process periodically. In the same manner we need to evaluate our belief systems periodically and allow our minds to think outside of our current realities.

Religious spirits love to condemn us for thinking outside of the box.

This is a counter-intuitive process. Religious spirits love to condemn us for thinking outside of the box. When we challenge the very things that we know for sure are true so we can pursue a higher revelation, the devil *is not* happy! He knows if we come to a higher understanding of who God is and what He has for our lives that it will bring destruction to his domain.

I want to give you peace of mind. God loved you before you knew Him; He will still love you when you know

Him—even when you allow your brain to challenge some of your core beliefs. He won't condemn you for using the brain He has given you. Even when we come to wrong conclusions, we can be assured that He will draw us back in: "*Your ears shall hear a word behind you, saying, 'This is the way, walk in it'*" (Isaiah 30:21, NIV).

If God loved us when we were in sin, He will surely love us now. Allow yourself to think bigger. Allow your brain to wander off and explore possibilities outside the box you've always been in. If you are wrong, that's fine. He'll call you back. But if you're right, the possibilities are endless.

Remember, you are called for greatness! You are called to have an abundant life. Let's escape the limitation and move beyond our current experience together.

Coaching Questions

1. In this chapter I talk about giving back all knowledge to the Lord in an effort to gain a greater understanding, even of the things we know for sure we are right on. What are some things that you know for sure that you can give back to the Lord for refinement or redefinition?

_____

_____

_____

_____

_____

_____

_____

2. I explained the prophetic message behind the Feast of Unleavened Bread and how it represents the removal of corrupted doctrine from our lives. This can be a scary thing. What are your biggest fears when it comes to entering this process? What are the things that keep you from celebrating the Feast of Unleavened Bread in your life?

_____

_____

_____

_____

_____

_____

_____

_____

chapter 7

Get Out!

WE HAVE NOW COVERED the first two steps of the five-step process that will help us get unboxed.

Step 1 was Awareness. We need to get an awareness that in fact there is a box—and an awareness of the reality that we actually might be in that box.

Step 2 was Thinking Bigger—encouraging us to think bigger than the box: What else is out there that I am missing? There must be more. Let's explore it. Let's think bigger and let's think beyond our current reality and experiences. Let's discover a page of new possibilities and opportunities that formerly couldn't be seen from within the box.

Now that we discovered new possibilities beyond our current reality it is important that we leave the boxes we're in.

There is no use for thinking outside the box and discovering a world that is out there, only to stay in the one that limits us. This may seem like a logical and simple conclusion to you, but this step can be harder than you think. There is a serious discrepancy between perceiving what needs to happen and actually making it happen by taking action.

You can dream all day long about possibilities outside of your current paradigm, but unless you have the courage to leave that paradigm it will only harm you.

Step 3: Take Action

Therefore, Step 3 is all about stepping out of the box by putting your faith into action.

Exploring new possibilities is great. But unless we have the courage to step out and actually do something, it's not going to help anyone. In fact, you can dream all day long about possibilities outside of your current paradigm, but unless you have the courage to leave that paradigm it will only harm you.

The Bible tells me the following: *"Hope deferred makes the heart sick, but a longing fulfilled is a tree of life"* (Proverbs 13:12, NIV).

Step 2 in the process is all about hope. When you can see outside of the limitations of your current reality, it creates hope. Hope is an amazingly powerful force but only if it is not deferred. If it is deferred, it makes the heart sick.

In order to prevent this from happening we need to put action to the vision developed during Step 2. Again, this sounds easier than it is. We are so ingrained with mind-sets, thought patterns, and habits that it can be extremely hard to break out. Our brains are pre-programmed to think the old way, which makes it extremely hard to break out.

In fact, the stronghold is in our mind:

The weapons we fight with are not the weapons of the world. On the contrary, they have divine power to demolish strongholds. We demolish arguments and every pretension that sets itself up against the knowledge of God, and we take captive every thought to make it obedient to Christ (2 Corinthians 10:4-5, NIV).

The knowledge of God is at war with the arguments that exalt themselves against it. The realm of thought, or, in other words, our mind, is the battlefield.

Step 3, then, is all about taking into captivity the wrong thoughts and mind-sets so we can be liberated to step outside of our comfort zone. Someone once said that you can never discover new oceans unless you actually have the courage to leave sight of the shore. That is so true. The shore is the safe place. The place we are familiar with. It's our comfort zone. What's more, discovering new territories and then actually taking possession of them would require making sure we have courage to leave the place we've become so familiar with.

Innovation and progress take place at the edge of chaos. It happens when familiar terrain meets unfamiliar terrain—a place that is not developed, a place of chaos where there is no order yet. When you find a place that is developed it means that someone went before you and brought order to it. What I am talking about here will help you find a place that is undeveloped and make it your own.

(Important): Believe You Are Unique—and Act On It

Remember the people of Israel. They came to the Jordan River, ready to take the Land. When they had crossed the river, something amazing happened. The land of promise across the Jordan had an allocated place for each individual. Every person who belonged to the nation of Israel had their own inheritance. No place was the same. Each person had a piece of land that was destined for him or her, that had their name written on it. No other person was supposed to take that piece of land. It was theirs.

Innovation and progress take place at the edge of chaos.

This reveals an amazing principle from the heart of God. He doesn't want your purpose and destiny to be the same as another person's. You are unique. By divine design each of us will always have to discover a new territory that is undeveloped. There is no point of reference in history of who you are destined to be. God created you with a divine destiny to possess a piece of land that belongs to you and you alone. To possess your land you will have to leave the box you grew up in.

The story of Elijah and Elisha illustrates the difference between seeing and doing. It perfectly describes a group of people who perceived the reality of the future yet chose to stay within the present because of the way their minds had been programmed. It contrasts that with the story of Elisha, who saw the same things these people saw but chose to deal with the information differently. He chose to act on what he saw rather than passively defaulting to what he was familiar with.

Let's read this story in 2 Kings 2:1-17 (NKJV):

And it came to pass, when the Lord was about to take up Elijah into heaven by a whirlwind, that Elijah went with Elisha from Gilgal. Then Elijah said to Elisha, "Stay here, please, for the Lord has sent me on to Bethel." But Elisha said, "As the Lord lives, and as your soul lives, I will not leave you!" So they went down to Bethel.

Now the sons of the prophets who were at Bethel came out to Elisha, and said to him, "Do you know that the Lord will take away your master from over you today?" And he said, "Yes, I know; keep silent!" Then Elijah said to him, "Elisha, stay here, please, for the Lord has sent me on to Jericho." But he said, "As the Lord lives, and as your soul lives, I will not leave you!" So they came to Jericho.

Now the sons of the prophets who were at Jericho came to Elisha and said to him, "Do you know that the Lord will take away your master from over you today?" So he answered, "Yes, I know; keep silent!" Then Elijah said to him, *"Stay here, please, for the Lord has sent me on to the Jordan."* But he said, *"As the Lord lives, and as your soul lives, I will not leave you!"*

So the two of them went on. And fifty men of the sons of the prophets went and stood facing them at a distance, while the two of them stood by the Jordan. Now Elijah took his mantle, rolled it up, and struck the water; and it was divided this way and that, so that the two of them crossed over on dry ground. And so it was, when they had crossed over, that Elijah said to Elisha, *"Ask! What may I do for you, before I am taken away from you?"* Elisha said, *"Please let a double portion of your spirit be upon me."*

So he said, *"You have asked a hard thing. Nevertheless, if you see me when I am taken from you, it shall be so for you; but if not, it shall not be so."* Then it happened, as they continued on and talked, that suddenly a chariot of fire appeared with horses of fire, and separated the two of them; and Elijah went up by a whirlwind into heaven.

And Elisha saw it, and he cried out, *"My father, my father, the chariot of Israel and its horsemen!"* So he saw him no more. And he took hold of his own clothes and *tore them into two pieces. He also took up the mantle of Elijah that had fallen from him, and went back and stood by the bank of the Jordan. Then he took the mantle of Elijah that had fallen from him, and struck the water, and said, "Where is the Lord God of Elijah?" And when he also had struck the water, it was divided this way and that; and Elisha crossed over.*

Now when the sons of the prophets who were from Jericho saw him, they said, "The spirit of Elijah rests on Elisha." And they came to meet him, and bowed to the ground before him. Then they said to him, "Look now, there are fifty strong men with your servants. Please let them go and search for your master, lest perhaps the Spirit of the Lord has taken him up and cast him upon some mountain or into some valley." And he said, "You shall not send anyone."

But when they urged him till he was ashamed, he said, "Send them!" Therefore they sent fifty men, and they searched for three days but did not find him. And when they came back to him, for he had stayed in Jericho, he said to them, "Did I not say to you, 'Do not go'?"

Here is the backstory. Elisha was about to be launched into his own unique, authentic ministry. He had been mentored/fathered by Elijah for quite some time. He had learned a lot. The time had come for Elisha to take over, as Elijah was about to leave. The manner by which he was to leave was quite remarkable as you can read in this story. I would say it was quite out-of-the-box!

Never before in history had anyone left earth in the manner that Elijah did. There had been one other person in history who technically never died; his name was Enoch: *"Enoch walked faithfully with God; then he was no more, because God took him away"* (Genesis 5:24, NIV).

However, this one was different. Chariots of fire? *Wow!* Who would have thought that was even within the realm of possibility? There was no point of reference whatsoever in all of history for something like that to happen.

Yet, for some reason, there were quite a few people who knew that it was going to happen. You see, once you master Step 1 and Step 2 in the process, you are able to see things others can't see within their current paradigm. That is exactly what happened in the story we just read.

Here is Elijah, and he is moving from the city of Gilgal to the city of Bethel. Before he departs he discourages Elisha to stay in Gilgal, yet Elisha doesn't want to hear it. He is committed to take action and follow his master.

Yet when he arrived in Bethel there was a group people, the sons of the prophets, who wanted to point out something to Elisha. They said, "Do you know that the Lord will take away your master from over you today?"

They saw the future, but their experience never became more than seeing.

Apparently this group of prophets was very accurate in anticipating the future. They were right. They foresaw the future. They knew exactly what was about to happen with Elijah, even though there was no point of reference in history for what was about to happen. I would say that was a pretty impressive prophetic gift they possessed, don't you think?

When they pointed this out to Elisha he said: "Yes, I know; keep silent!" Elisha had seen the exact same thing the prophets had seen. They both had reached Step 2 in the process. They had perceived a reality outside of their box.

The story continues by Elijah telling Elisha that he's going to Jericho. The scenario repeats itself except for one difference. The prophets stay behind. They don't follow Elijah; they stay in Bethel. There was no action taken on the revelation. They saw the future, but their experience never became more than seeing.

Upon arriving in Jericho another company of prophets appeared on the scene. They had seen the same thing as Elisha. They even pointed it out to Elisha that Elijah was going to be taken away. Very impressive prophetic revelation, wouldn't you say? They could see very clearly outside of the box of their current reality by declaring those words. Yet, when Elijah left Jericho, they stayed behind. Their revelation never became more than information pertaining to the future. They were never part of it because they stayed at a distance!

Elisha refused to be that way. He was committed to the process. He knew that action needed to be added to the revelation if he was going to see different results in his ministry. So when Elijah discouraged him to stay in Jericho he said: "As the Lord lives, and as your soul lives, I will not leave you!" The courage to act on what he saw was the key to Elisha's release into his own unique, authentic ministry.

Faith + No Works = Zero

The same is true for us. We need to act on what the Lord shows us. Faith without works is dead (James 2:26).

Here are some of the interesting points in this story:

Every city Elijah and Elisha traveled to had a bunch of people who perceived and saw the future accurately. They knew exactly what was about to happen. I would say that that is pretty impressive. My point here is that Elisha was not the only one who could see beyond the present into the future. He was not the only one who saw things outside of the box or the current reality.

Yet, he was the only one who actually took action on what he saw.

For me, however, there is a way more interesting detail in the story. It pertains to the other guys, the prophets who were right all along but never took action. Think about this for a moment. Here are a bunch of guys—we don't know how many, but my guess is there were at least 150 of them who saw into the future prophetically and accurately. They perceived and declared the very thing that God was about to do with Elijah.

You would think that when this actually did happen that they would be the ones saying, "Told you so!" Yet their response was completely the opposite of that. Isn't that crazy? They were the ones who collectively prophesied and declared what was about to happen to Elijah. Yet when their words came to pass, something really remarkable happened. They were the ones who said in verse 16 of this story: "Look now, there are fifty strong men with your servants. Please let them go and search for your master, lest perhaps the Spirit of the Lord has taken him up and cast him upon some mountain or into some valley."

Once the opportunity presents itself, we actually will need to have the courage to leave our existing paradigm and venture into that new territory.

Wow! Isn't that crazy? The ones who foretold the future were the very ones who instantly defaulted back to their past experiences and reality. Their first reaction was to send out fifty delegates into the mountains to try to recover the very thing they said would go away.

Let me say this again: Their immediate instinct was to recover the very thing they declared would go away based on what they had seen pertaining the future!

Just thinking and seeing outside of the box is not enough. Once the opportunity presents itself, we actually will need to have the courage to leave our existing paradigm and venture into that new territory you've been seeing for a while.

We all are in danger of not doing this. We all are prone to stick with what we know. We may perceive the world that God has in store for us outside the norm, but when it comes down to it, *are we taking action on what we see, or are we defaulting back to what we know?*

I don't know about you, but I want to be like Elijah and say: "As the Lord lives, and as your soul lives, I will not leave you!"

When we think outside of the box and discover a whole new world is out there, I pray we will have the courage to take the action that goes with the discovery!

As for me, I want to get out of the box! How about you?

Coaching Questions

1. What practical steps can you take to put action to what you discovered on your journey so far? What are some things that God has shown you in the process of this book that you can now put to action by making some clear decisions?

_____

_____

_____

_____

_____

_____

_____

2. In this chapter I make a comparison between the company of prophets and Elisha. Do you identify more with Elisha or with the company of prophets? Why? If you identify more with the company of prophets, what practical decisions can you make in order to change that?

chapter 8

Destroy the Box

WELL, HERE WE ARE! Step 4 of the process. This step is probably the most difficult one in the process, but it is likely to also be the step that produces the most freedom in your life. Don't get me wrong, thinking and stepping outside the box can be very liberating. However, just because you are now outside the box doesn't mean the box cannot control you.

Something else will need to happen in order for you to "seal the deal," something that deals with the boxes of your past, once and for all. You see, once you leave your box, that box is still part of your world. You may be outside of it, but it's almost like the box is still at the center of your thinking. It's like you are tied to it with an invisible string.

Mind-sets, paradigms, culture, and thought processes are very powerful, as we have seen in the last chapter. If the fifty prophets were unable to shake off what they knew from past experiences, what makes us think that we can? What makes us think that we too will not default back to what we've always known as "right"?

Step 4: Destroy Your Box

Something else will need to happen in order to establish yourself in your newfound freedom. You are going to need to destroy your box and remove it from your reality completely—in fact, any and all boxes from your past. Somehow you are going to have to destroy those boxes that once controlled your thinking and limited the abundant life that God has destined you for.

This is not an easy task, believe me! Once you start you'll find out quickly enough that these boxes don't go up in flames easily when you put fire to them. They are almost flame-retardant! They are hard to destroy. Yet, somehow, we all must go through this phase in order to experience true freedom.

But take hope, for there is a place where the box no longer exercises control over your life. Sure, you will still live in a world where people have boxes. That will never change.

But you will eventually come to a place where your box no longer exercises control over you. When you are able to destroy your box, you will be truly free to go in and out of other people's boxes without being affected by them.

You are going to need to destroy your box and remove it from your reality completely.

Why must we be so determined to destroy our boxes? Because getting out of your box without destroying it creates a polarizing environment in which you develop what I call "anti-behavior" against the box you once were part of. You develop an attitude "against" something you were once part of. You position yourself as the "alternative" to a world you worked so hard to leave. This doesn't produce freedom. It actually keeps you in bondage to the box. Even though you may be out of it, you are still controlled by its presence. Maybe not from within, but you're always using that world you were once part of as a reference to show the alternative.

I know—this is some deep stuff. Let's read a scripture so I can clarify what I mean in more detail:

Now when Joshua was near Jericho, he looked up and saw a man standing in front of him with a drawn sword in his hand. Joshua went up to him and asked, "Are you for us or for our enemies?" "Neither," he replied, "but as commander of the army of the Lord I have now come." Then Joshua fell facedown to the ground in reverence, and asked him, "What message does my Lord[a] have for his servant?" (Joshua 5:13-14, NIV)

Joshua had just taken over leadership from his predecessor, Moses, who remained on the other side of the Jordan. Moses had just passed away, and Joshua was chosen to lead God's people into the Promised Land. That was not an easy task. Remember, forty years earlier Joshua had been among the twelve spies who had scouted out the land. It was he along with his friend Caleb who, despite the fact that there were giants in the land, had advised the people that with God on their side they would be more than able to conquer Canaan. However, the word and recommendation of the other ten spies had outweighed theirs As a result, God had sent the entire nation back into the wilderness for forty years because they chose not to believe God's promise that He had given them the land.

Now four decades later, Joshua and Caleb were back. They were the only two survivors from their generation. The land that had been promised to them all those years before was finally within reach. There was just a little detail that had to be sorted out. It was called Jericho!

Jericho was a fortified city just across the Jordan. It was the first city of many that had to be conquered in order for Israel to possess the promise God had given them. No easy task to take Jericho, considering its fortified walls and the incredible strength this city displayed. Jericho had a reputation. Jericho was not a city that was easily taken.

One morning, Joshua stood on a hill outside of the city praying to the Lord about the almost impossible task that was ahead of them. A man walked up to him who had a drawn sword in his hand. As he stood opposite of Joshua, Joshua walked over to him and asked him a question that revealed something profound about Joshua.

"Are you for us or for our adversaries?" Joshua asked the man.

Think about this for a minute. This was the mighty Joshua. He had survived forty years of wilderness. One by one he saw his peers die over the course of those years, yet somehow he survived. God had a plan for him. He had a promise that one day Joshua would take the land that He was promised.

But just because God had a plan for Joshua, didn't mean that Joshua was exempt from having a wrong mind-set. Just because he was promised Canaan didn't mean that he wasn't subject to thinking in boxes.

Why Boxes Limit Your Options

Joshua's response was rooted in a polarizing mind-set that allowed for only two options. *Are you for us? Or are you against us?* He couldn't think beyond those two options. Those two boxes controlled the realm of possibility from where he was standing.

Our little self-fabricated truths keep us from thinking bigger and beyond.

Joshua's mind-set was governed by those boxes, and he didn't allow any space for a third, fourth, or even fifth option. Could it be that the boxes he had created for himself were completely irrelevant within the context of God's vantage point?

I believe the latter is true. Where Joshua (or you and me) tend to think within a limited number of possibilities, God always thinks bigger. In His mind, our little self-fabricated truths keep us from thinking bigger and beyond.

In Joshua's case, God's answer was profound. His response to the question of whether He was "for" or "against" Joshua and the people was "Yes."

The man who appeared to be sent from God, the commander of the army of the Lord, completely destroyed Joshua's paradigm by answering him this way, showing him the irrelevance of Joshua's question. If we don't destroy the box from our thinking—completely—then we are in danger of the same assumption Joshua made. It's the assumption that there are two options placed against each other as polar opposites.

True freedom comes, however, when you are able to remove the relevance of that polarizing mind-set. It's not one or the other. In the same way the man revealed to Joshua the ridiculousness of his question by answering yes to an either/or question, we too need to come to the place where the world we once were part of no longer exists in our thinking.

Again, I know this is deep stuff, and I hope and pray I am somehow able to convey the depth of this liberating truth to you effectively. I'll give you another example before moving on.

The truth is that we all have to deal with something that is trying to keep us in a place where we choose between two polarizing options. That's our nature. That's what the fall of mankind has given us. Remember where it all went wrong? Let's read it:

And the Lord God commanded the man, "You are free to eat from any tree in the garden; but you must not eat from the tree of the knowledge of good and evil, for when you eat from it you will certainly die" (Genesis 2:16-17, NIV).

God placed man in the garden amid thousands of trees. He commanded them to eat from any tree they wanted to, except one. It was the tree that would give them knowledge of two polarizing options: good and evil.

You see, before they ate from that tree they didn't have knowledge of good and evil. They simply knew something far more profound and beneficial. All they knew was life!

In the middle of the garden were the tree of life and the tree of the knowledge of good and evil (Genesis 2:9, NIV).

Good and evil became a replacement of life the moment Adam and Eve chose to eat from that tree. They suddenly started to think in those two boxes instead of the higher way of thinking, which was rooted in life.

God had said that the knowledge of good and evil would produce death, and it did. In fact, it still does today. Our default instinct is to judge everything around us and separate it into two categories. Instead of asking ourselves what would bring life to a situation, we tend to put everything into one of two boxes: good or evil.

Religion sucks the life out of any situation and replaces it with something that produces death.

Apparently it's possible to have knowledge of what is good and still produce death. That's what religion does. It sucks the life out of any situation and replaces it with something that produces death. Therefore, we need to come to a place where we can destroy the boxes we've created in our minds and allow the Lord to replace it with a "tree of life" that will put us into a situation where we can see far beyond what we could see before, thus producing life. Even when we deal with people who might still be part of a paradigm we were once part of, instead of antagonizing them with "the alternative option," we can approach them on a higher level by allowing life to flow through us without adding a sense of condemnation or pointing fingers. The box has to become irrelevant by being destroyed and removed from our thinking altogether.

God loves to destroy things that keep us from experiencing the abundant life He has for us.

I know what you are thinking. "Destroying" sounds so aggressive. It's so radical. It implies that there is a "point of no return"—which, by the way, is another reason we should destroy the box. As long as the box is still within your proximity, the temptation to jump right back in remains.

God loves to destroy things that keep us from experiencing the abundant life He has for us. In fact, from time to time He calls people with a specific purpose to destroy the things that stand in the way of the advancement of His kingdom.

For example, let's look at the prophetic destiny of the one of the prophets of the Old Testament, Jeremiah.

Then the word of the Lord came to me, saying: "Before I formed you in the womb I knew you; Before you were born I sanctified you; I ordained you a prophet to the nations." Then said I: "Ah, Lord God! Behold, I cannot speak, for I am a youth." But the Lord said to me: "Do not say, 'I am a youth,' for you shall go to all to whom I send you, and whatever I command you, you shall speak. Do not be afraid of their faces, for I am with you to deliver you," says the Lord. Then the Lord put forth His hand and touched my mouth, and the Lord said to me: "Behold, I have put My words in your mouth. See, I have this day set you over the nations and over the kingdoms, to root out and to pull down, to destroy and to throw down, to build and to plant" (Jeremiah 1:5-10, NKJV).

The very purpose and calling on the life of the prophet Jeremiah was to destroy. This was something determined before he was even formed in the womb. *Wow!* God actually called Jeremiah to be a destroyer before he was born.

Obviously there was a purpose to the destruction that Jeremiah was supposed to bring, which was to build and to plant (v.10). However, look at the "balance" between the words God used to describe Jeremiah's calling.

He says that He called Jeremiah to do six things:

- Root out
- Pull Down
- Destroy
- Throw Down
- Build
- Plant

Jeremiah received six prophetic declarations that would define his ministry, four of which are negative and two positive. This reveals the priority as well as the difficulty of removing/destroying the negative before the positive can be done. In other words, Jeremiah's gifting was focused twice as much on dismantling the negative as on bringing the positive.

There's No Such Thing as 'Partial Destruction'

The same is true in context of what we are talking about in this chapter. There is no use for "building" and "planting" if we do not first deal with the destroying of the boxes and mind-sets that have become so embedded in our lives.

Building and planting is easy, but only after the ground has first been cultivated.

Remember, it's possible for God's people (you and me) to build, plan, and work hard, yet only produce pyramids. We need to destroy and remove all boxes from our thinking before moving into Step 5 of the process.

It's possible for God's people (you and me) to build, plan, and work hard, yet only produce pyramids.

Now before we go into Step 5, I will make this "destruction" of our past realities a bit more real. I'll do that by telling you a couple of different stories from the Bible. The first is from the life of King David. One night while he was lying in bed, he received inspiration from God:

After the king was settled in his palace and the Lord had given him rest from all his enemies around him, he said to Nathan the prophet, "Here I am, living in a house of cedar, while the ark of God remains in a tent" (2 Samuel 7:1-2, NIV).

David came up with the idea to build God a temple. Up to that point in time, the Ark of God had been in a tent called the Tabernacle. Then, in 1 Chronicles, it is revealed that David isn't to build this temple because there was too much blood on his hands.

But God said to me, "You are not to build a house for my Name, because you are a warrior and have shed blood" (1 Chronicles 28:3, NIV).

As a result, his son King Solomon ended up building the temple:

"In the four hundred and eightieth year after the Israelites came out of Egypt, in the fourth year of Solomon's reign over Israel, in the month of Ziv, the second month, he began to build the temple of the Lord" (1 Kings 6:1, NIV).

It took king Solomon many years to complete the temple. Just think about it: blood, sweat, tears, plus all the gold and silver used to complete the structure. It was quite the undertaking. It wasn't a quick "filler project" that he did to kill some time. There was a serious emotional and financial investment required to complete the task.

Then after years of building the temple, it was finally completed and the Ark of the Covenant was brought into the Holy of Holies inside the temple:

So all the work that Solomon had done for the house of the Lord was finished; and Solomon brought in the things which his father David had dedicated: the silver and the gold and all the furnishings. And he put them in the treasuries of the house of God. Now Solomon assembled the elders of Israel and all the heads of the tribes, the chief fathers of the children of Israel, in Jerusalem, that they might bring the ark of the covenant of the Lord up from the City of David, which is Zion. Therefore all the men of Israel assembled with the king at the feast, which was in the seventh month. So all the elders of Israel came, and the Levites took up the ark. Then they brought up the ark, the tabernacle of meeting, and all the holy furnishings that were in the tabernacle. The priests and the Levites brought them up. Also King Solomon, and all the congregation of Israel who were assembled with him before the ark, were sacrificing sheep and oxen that could not be counted or numbered for multitude. Then the priests brought in the ark of the covenant of the Lord to its place, into the inner sanctuary of the temple, to the Most Holy Place, under the wings of the cherubim. For the cherubim spread their wings over the place of the ark, and the cherubim overshadowed the ark and its poles. The poles extended so that the ends of the poles of the ark could be seen from the holy place, in front of the inner sanctuary; but they could not be seen from outside. And they are there to this day. Nothing was in the ark except the two tablets which Moses put there at Horeb, when the Lord made a covenant with the children of Israel, when they had come out of Egypt.

And it came to pass when the priests came out of the Most Holy Place (for all the priests who were present had sanctified themselves, without keeping to their divisions), and the Levites who were the singers, all those of Asaph and Heman and Jeduthun, with their sons and their brethren, stood at the east end of the altar, clothed in white linen, having cymbals, stringed instruments and harps, and with them one hundred and twenty priests sounding with trumpets—indeed it came to pass, when the trumpeters and singers were as one, to make one sound to be heard in praising and thanking the Lord, and when they lifted up their voice with the trumpets and cymbals and instruments of music, and praised the Lord, saying: "For He is good, for His mercy endures forever," then the house, the house of the Lord, was filled with a cloud, so that the priests could not continue ministering because of the cloud; for the glory of the Lord filled the house of God (2 Chronicles 5:1-14, NKJV).

Wow! What a story! I would say that Solomon's project was quite a success story. Pretty amazing. It took a while to complete it and cost a bit of effort and money; but, hey, it was all worth it. In fact, as they finished the temple and allowed the Ark to be ushered in, God showed up in a cloud. Can you imagine? None of the priests were able to minister because of the glory of the Lord that filled the temple.

But it didn't end there! That was just the beginning. Now that the temple was completed and considered a success story, it continued to become the epic center of religious activity of the nation of Israel for centuries after. For almost 1,000 years, the temple was the place to be when it came to religious activity in Israel. Several times a year everyone traveled to Jerusalem for all kinds of festivities that took place around the temple. If someone sinned, they could bring an animal and sacrifice it to be forgiven. All spiritual activity of God's people seemed to be centered around that temple.

And what started it all? Divine inspiration received by King David and executed by his son King Solomon. Who inspired all this? God did!

Be Willing to Let Go

Now that you have this picture in your mind, let's fast-forward 1,000 years. The same God who kept David up that night inspiring him about the temple inspired someone else. The same God inspired Jesus, who was sent by Him to take His people beyond their current experience into a place far beyond it.

Jesus showed up one day at that same temple and looked around. And that same God who inspired construction of the temple and placed His hand on it for centuries upon centuries, inspired Jesus to make a statement that utterly shocked and offended the religious order of the day!

Jesus said: *"I will destroy this temple made with human hands and in three days will build another, not made with hands"* (Mark 14:58, NIV).

Wow! What a "contradiction." At least it appears to be a contradiction, if all you can do is think inside of one box. Apparently it is possible for God to inspire something at one point and have it be a blessing to many, only to inspire someone later to destroy it! Pretty crazy, right?

His kingdom is ever increasing, and He wants to use you and me to co-labor with Him in accomplishing just that.

Here was Jesus, sent by God with an assignment to destroy the very thing God inspired King David to build! This kind of stuff messes with your mind, doesn't it? The only reason it messes with your mind is because we tend to think in boxes. We tend to establish a paradigm about something and anchor it into eternity. Yet God wants to bring us from glory to glory and strength to strength. He doesn't want to keep us where we were yesterday. He wants to move things forward. He wants to advance our lives, our ministry, and His kingdom.

In fact, He wants to use you and me to accomplish just that. His kingdom is ever increasing, and He wants to use you and me to co-labor with Him in accomplishing just that. The growth of His kingdom on earth cannot stop. The increase of His kingdom cannot stall: *"Of the increase of His government and peace there will be no end"* (Isaiah 9:7, NIV).

Jesus doesn't destroy without a purpose. He destroys so that he can rebuild something.

But it requires us to be open-minded enough to have Jesus show up on our "temple squares" to destroy the very things we've assumed were eternal. Could it be that Jesus shows up in our churches, lives, and ministries today to destroy the very things we've toiled and worked for so long, simply to open up possibilities for greater opportunities beyond our current realities?

I believe it is! He apparently did it before.

We have to understand one thing, though. Jesus doesn't destroy without a purpose. He destroys so that he can rebuild something. Remember, Jesus said that "within three days I will build another temple." He was talking about a temple built of living stones that would take His plan with creation to the next level.

The only thing needed to enable that to happen was to strip away the paradigm that the "temple service" God's people had for centuries been so accustomed to had lost its validity. Jesus had to "destroy" the box first before He could create something new.

Now, just to show you how profound all of this is, let's go quickly to the book of Acts, where we can read the final words that Jesus spoke on Earth before He went to His Father.

But you will receive power when the Holy Spirit comes on you; and you will be my witnesses in Jerusalem, and in all Judea and Samaria, and to the ends of the earth (Acts 1:8, NIV).

Now, remember, these were the last words Jesus spoke. In other words, if there was ever a time to pay attention to what Jesus had to say, THEN was that time. After that, there would be no further words to be heard from Jesus. That was it. His final speech before, "Good-bye!" It wasn't just a kitchen-table conversation. It was His final speech. If I had been there listening to this, I would have taken notes for sure!

Remember, Jesus had made it very clear that this Temple in Jerusalem was "destroyed." Meaning, God had already been relegated it to the past. It was done. Maybe it wasn't physically destroyed at that point, but the power of it had already been lifted. That happened the moment John the Baptist declared that Jesus was the Lamb of God when He showed up to be baptized by John: *"The next day John saw Jesus coming toward him and said, 'Look, the Lamb of God, who takes away the sin of the world!'"* (John 1:29, NIV).

For centuries, lambs were slaughtered in the Temple to represent redemption and the forgiveness of sin. This "system" worked for many years—and it was God's system—but when Jesus showed up that day and John prophetically declared that Jesus was now that Lamb of God, the power of the system was lifted and placed on Christ.

All the disciples were part of this experience. They knew who Jesus was and what He had come to accomplish. They knew what the Temple meant. And now the power of the Temple had officially been lifted. They now lived in a new paradigm. Or did they?

I mean, the mandate Jesus gave during His final speech was very clear: "The ends of the earth"! They were not to stay in Jerusalem. Even though that's where their calling in

God had started and where they had experienced tremendous spiritual success, they couldn't stay there. They had to become witnesses to Him far beyond the walls of Jerusalem, in Judea, Samaria, and even to the ends of the earth.

Once you have established a "box" in your thinking, it is very hard to get rid of it.

It doesn't matter how you listen to those final words of Jesus. There could be interpreted in only one way. They had to go into the whole world, reaching each corner of the earth and becoming a witness wherever they went.

However, wrong paradigms are a hard nut to crack. Once you have established a "box" in your thinking, it is very hard to get rid of it. It's one thing to know that there is a box, in theory, and a world beyond that reality. But it's something else to actually destroy it from your daily experience.

Again, how many interpretations could there possibly be when it comes to Jesus' last words? Not many! How many ways can you interpret "the ends of the earth." Pretty clear, right?

The challenge, however, is the established paradigm in the minds of the apostles. If for so many years you've carried a "temple mentality" that has been rooted in your thinking, then it is going to be very hard to move forward with instructions that can only be followed if you destroy the outdated paradigm.

If the apostles struggled to leave behind the box from the past, what makes us think we're exempt from the same deception?

The same held true for the disciples. If anyone should have known the "right thing to do" it was them. Yet they failed to destroy the box that kept them in their past. This is what happened: "*On that day a great persecution broke out against the church in Jerusalem, and all except the apostles were scattered throughout Judea and Samaria*" (Acts 8:1, NIV).

That is a piece of very interesting history. It talks about persecution coming against the church, which caused a tremendous dispersion of the believers into different regions.

The Christians all were scattered *except* for the apostles! They stayed in Jerusalem. Not only did they not leave Jerusalem, but guess where they chose to meet every day? That's right. Their preferred place to meet every day was the very place Jesus had come to destroy!

Day after day, in the temple courts and from house to house, they never stopped teaching and proclaiming the good news that Jesus is the Messiah (Acts 5:42, NIV).

Can you believe it! Not only did they allow their outdated paradigm to keep them from fulfilling the apostolic mandate Jesus had given them, but they also chose the very place Jesus came to destroy as one of their primary locations to meet.

They met at the Temple—daily! Pretty crazy, right?

If the apostles struggled to leave behind the box from the past, what makes us think we're exempt from the same deception? We're not! Like them, we are lured into believing that the ways of the past are still relevant in the future, despite other signals that the Lord may have given us.

The interesting thing in the lives of the early apostles was that it took the actual destruction of the temple in A.D. 70 to finally mobilize them to move beyond the walls of Jerusalem and reach the corners of the earth. After the temple was actually destroyed and removed from their proximity, they really no longer had a choice. There was no Temple! This fact finally propelled them into fulfilling the instruction the Lord had given them.

Let us be aware of the same dynamic so we can avoid the same mistakes they made. Let's destroy the boxes from our world that keep us locked in limitation and the past. Let's avoid desperate measures and a physical destruction by allowing the Lord to remove each box completely from our thinking so we are free to actually fulfill what He has mandated for us to do.

Let's destroy the box! Because when we do, we will finally be ready for the next and final step in the process. It not only will rock your world, but also the world of those around you.

Coaching Questions

1. Are there any areas in your life in which you feel like you've been feeding from the wrong tree? Where have you replaced the tree of life with the tree of knowledge of good and evil? What practical steps can you take in order to change that?

_____

_____

_____

_____

_____

_____

_____

2. What temple mentality keeps you stuck in the past? What mindset is keeping you from fulfilling your true mandate?

_____

_____

_____

_____

_____

_____

_____

_____

chapter 9

Create

Y OU ARE MADE FOR SO MUCH MORE! You are created and destined to have an abundant life that God has prepared for you. As we discovered already, there is an enemy that tries to keep you from ever reaching the ultimate goal He has prepared for you. His tactic is to make us believe that the life we have today is in fact the abundant life the Bible talks about. His strongest weapon is to convince us to believe that the life we live is the life we're going to live until we die. It's the biggest and most dangerous lie we can ever believe, yet the tragedy is that most of us have fallen into that trap and believe it.

Over the last four chapters, we've systematically dismantled that lie. We've done so by embarking on a

153

journey of unboxing your life by making you aware of this tactic, as well as a world of abundance that exists beyond your current reality. We have seen that when you allow yourself to think bigger than what you are experiencing today, you'll actually start to see some of the things that God has in store for you that you couldn't see from your previous vantage point. Once we see this and develop the courage to believe it, we then need to act, stepping out into those new territories that were previously hidden from our reality.

There are so many sides to God's creative expression that it would be impossible for one man to determine the parameters of what this could look like.

When we step out of that box and embrace the vision and dream God has for our lives, amazing things can happen. Yet unless we destroy the box we once were part of, we will never experience the fullness of what is about to happen in Step 5.

Step 5: Create

Step 5 is all about creating something. No, not a box again, but something that can only be authentically defined by you. It can be a lonely process because only you and you alone can take this part of the journey.

Remember when we talked about the unlimited spectrum of creativity that God had within Himself and how we tend to turn that into a limited set of predefined templates through which He can manifest Himself? In other words, we tend to create boxes of limitations through which God is "allowed" to manifest Himself, and we call it "ministry."

However, this is what the Bible teaches us:

"Although I am less than the least of all the Lord's people, this grace was given me: to preach to the Gentiles the boundless riches of Christ, and to make plain to everyone the administration of this mystery, which for ages past was kept hidden in God, who created all things. His intent was that now, through the church, the manifold wisdom of God should be made known to the rulers and authorities in the heavenly realms, according to his eternal purpose that he accomplished in Christ Jesus our Lord" (Ephesians 3:8-11, NIV).

It doesn't talk about a "singular" wisdom; it talks about a wisdom that is "manifold." There are so many sides to God's creative expression that it would be impossible for one man to determine the parameters of what this could look like. In fact, collectively as human beings, we would not be able to define the boundaries of the potential of His creative expression, as He does more than what we can even think or imagine.

Yet when we look at our churches, ministries, projects, and events, they all seem to look the same.

In our "boxed" mind-sets we tend to create ministry templates that allow God to work through us in a very limited set of rules that we created for Him. Those templates and parameters of ministry that we have defined may make up only a sliver of the potential spectrum of possibility within God's reality.

Yet when we look at our churches, ministries, projects, and events, they all seem to look the same. Why is this? It's because we all tend to fall into a deception that keeps us from seeing the full reality of the manifold wisdom of God.

Uniformity is not a virtue. The devil will make you believe it is, but it isn't. It may have the appearance of a form of godliness, but it has denied the power thereof. I discovered this truth several years ago when I was teaching at a Bible college in Aruba, a small island in the Caribbean about forty miles from the coast of Venezuela.

I was teaching on some of the same things that I'm talking about in this book, explaining how so much or our everyday experience is determined by our limited paradigms on who God is and how He would like us to behave. I taught on this for five days. During those five days the church on the island had organized a March for Jesus event through the main streets of the island. Aruba is very small and has only about 110,000 people, with only one major town where most of the people live. The island is about seven miles wide and only about three to four miles deep. The churches had collectively decided that it would be a great idea and statement of unity to march around the city, holding banners and singing songs about Jesus.

I remember standing by the side of the road as hundreds of people marched through the streets. They all were wearing red T-shirts, singing the same songs, marching on the same beat and carrying the same smiles on their faces. I guess their goal was to show the love of Jesus through these efforts in hopes that others would be attracted to this display of "happiness and joy."

Now I have no doubt that the people in this march were marching with a pure heart and an upright motivation. I honestly believe that. Yet something was terribly off as I watched the crowds walk by. It seemed so forced. It seemed fake. It felt like it lacked authenticity. Their imposed behavior of walking, singing, and smiling a certain way appeared to have the opposite effect of what they were trying to accomplish.

God is not looking for uniformity! He's looking for diversity.

The random bystander on the street was certainly not attracted by their behavior. In fact, they often looked away in hopes that nobody would hand them one of those balloons or tracts they were passing out.

The Way of the Kingdom: Becoming Unique, Authentic Expressions

Suddenly it hit me. God is not looking for uniformity! He's looking for diversity. He is looking for an expression of His manifold wisdom through each and every individual in a unique way. Instead of trying to make us all do the same thing, He wants us all to start to do something different.

This was a real eye-opener for me. For so long I was taught that true unity was created through uniformity. Yet in that moment I started to see the difference between the two and realized that, in fact, the opposite is true. True unity is not accomplished through uniformity; it is accomplished through diversity.

We read this scripture in the Bible, which talks about this:

They run like mighty men,
They climb the wall like men of war;
Every one marches in formation,
And they do not break ranks.
They do not push one another;
Every one marches in his own column.
Though they lunge between the weapons,
They are not cut down.

They run to and fro in the city,
They run on the wall;
They climb into the houses,
They enter at the windows like a thief.
The earth quakes before them,
The heavens tremble;
The sun and moon grow dark,
And the stars diminish their brightness.
The Lord gives voice before His army,
For His camp is very great;
For strong is the One who executes His word (Joel 2:7-11, NIV).

This scripture describes the army of the Lord the way it is supposed to be. Each person in this army does not break rank. Each one marches in his own column. Nobody pushes each other.

In other words, everyone will be in their own lane, doing their own unique thing, without competing for the same space. And in doing so, they are being one. Unity is the result of each individual finding their own unique place within that army. No rank is the same. No position is equal. It's all uniquely designed for each individual to march in. And as we march in that unique, authentic spot, we become one.

Unity is not created through uniformity. In fact, uniformity creates an environment of competition where we all compete for the same thing. When we all realize that what I have to bring to the table is unique to me, I keep myself from trying to become someone (or something) else.

Unity is not created through uniformity. In fact, uniformity creates an environment of competition where we all compete for the same thing.

This chapter is all about finding your rank. This phase in the process of unboxing is all about finding your lane. If uniformity is the goal, I will always strive to become the best uniform me that I can be. It's like an army of soldiers who all look the same but one might have shinier shoes than the others. One might have a slightly better ironed shirt or fewer smudges on their uniform. There might be marginal differences, but there is nothing that makes us unique in that scenario.

It's all about giving birth to the very thing that God created you to give birth to. Something so unique that it doesn't have a point of reference anywhere else. Nobody else ever gave birth to what you are supposed to give birth to through your life.

We should have a blank canvas before we start to paint.

This is something that often is not promoted in our churches. Well, maybe it is in theory, but not in practice. More often than not we operate in wineskins, structures, and leadership models that don't facilitate an environment that creates a platform for this to happen.

That's why we need to remove "the box" first. The box determines and dictates the environment in which this process should take place in a limited way. It can't facilitate a structure that will make it happen.

We should have a blank canvas before we start to paint. That's why we went through the un-boxing process the way we did. Now that our canvas is completely empty, we can start creating.

So here we go!

There is this super interesting story in the Bible that talks about a conversation Peter had one day with Jesus. It's from the 18th chapter of Matthew. Let's read it.

When Jesus came into the region of Caesarea Philippi, He asked His disciples, saying, "Who do men say that I, the Son of Man, am?" So they said, "Some say John the Baptist, some Elijah, and others Jeremiah or one of the prophets." He said to them, "But who do you say that I am?" Simon Peter answered and said, "You are the Christ, the Son of the living God." Jesus answered and said to him, "Blessed are you, Simon Bar-Jonah, for flesh and blood has not revealed this to you, but My Father who is in heaven. And I also say to you that you are Peter, and on this rock I will build My church, and the gates of Hades shall not prevail against it (Matthew 18:13-18, NKJV).

I had heard this story many times. I thought it was a cool story, don't get me wrong; but after hearing it one too many times I started to get bored with it. How many times can you listen to the same sermon without getting bored?

My boredom was short-lived after I suddenly got a revelation from this portion of scripture which I had never seen

before. In fact, it revolutionized the way I look at things forever. Let's paraphrase the story a little bit as we unpack it.
Jesus is sitting down with Peter one day as they are having a
conversation. Jesus asks him:

"Hey Peter, tell me, what is the word on the street?"

Peter answered: "What do you mean, Lord?"

*Jesus: "Well, who do the people say I am? Tell me, what
stories are being told about who I am. What's the word
on the street?"*

*Peter: "Well, actually, there are quite a few stories going
around about you, Lord. Some say that you're John the
Baptist who came back from the dead. Others say you're
Elijah or one of the prophets. I can't really answer that
question since there are many, many stories going around
from different people expressing different opinions!"*

Jesus' question and Peter's answer is what I call a first-level
understanding (or revelation) that we all have at one point
in our walk with Christ. There is nothing wrong with it. In
fact, there is a time in your walk with God when you simply
believe what other people say about Jesus. When you just
become a believer, you simply believe what the pastor tells

you about who Jesus is. Nothing wrong with that. That's where we all start. We take other people's opinions and convictions and make them our own, based on what we've been told about Him. Not because we have our own revelation; we simply take other people's convictions and make them our own.

It's a healthy thing to get this first-level revelation. Everyone will have it at some point. It becomes a problem only when we stagnate and stay at that level. You see, there is a higher level of revelation we all need to get to at some point in our walk with the Lord. Let's look at this level-two revelation next.

Jesus: "Well, Peter, now that you know what other people say, let me ask you another question: Who do you say that I am?"

Wow. The questioning became a lot more personal. It no longer mattered what others had told Peter. It was now up to him to tap into a higher level of understanding to answer that question with boldness. So Peter answered:

Peter: "You, sir, are the Christ! You are the son of the living God!"

Jesus: "Oh, wow, Peter! I'm impressed. This is some information that you didn't get off the street. This is not something that anyone has told you. This is pure revelation that comes from the Father. He Himself must have revealed this to you because this is some information that wasn't public."

When Christ is revealed to us on a personal level, that revelation becomes more real than any circumstance and reality around us.

Now, remember, when Peter answered this question it wasn't public knowledge that Jesus was the Son of God. Nobody really knew who Jesus was at that point in time. In other words, the information Peter shared in answering Jesus' question was the result of a supernatural experience he'd had with the Father. Peter had been given a revelation from God Himself showing him that Jesus was the Christ, the Son of the living God!

Pretty amazing, isn't it? Peter heard from God about who Jesus truly was! This was another level of revelation and understanding that went far beyond what was heard in the streets. It was supernatural. It was personal. It was a real game-changer for Peter.

When Christ is revealed to us on a personal level, that revelation becomes more real than any circumstance and reality around us. When information turns into supernatural revelation, that reality surpasses everything around you, and you can truly start your walk with God.

And that's exactly what it is. You *start* your walk with God. This level *cannot* be our end goal. It's merely the starting point that will put you on a path leading you to a third level of revelation that nobody ever seems to talk about.

You see, most of our church culture is created to get people to that second level of revelation. As leaders we tend to make it our ultimate goal to help each and every person to get a revelation of Jesus on a supernatural level. We somehow have come to believe that once people get to this level they have arrived.

Guess what? It's not true. It's not true at all!

I honestly believe that by making this second-level revelation our primary goal it will distract the church from truly being victorious. Why? Because on this level, we all are equal. Though necessary, this second level of revelation becomes the breeding ground for uniformity if we stay there too long.

Don't get me wrong—we all need to have this second level of revelation. At some point we all have to move from other people's opinions into a pure revelatory conviction that is personal.

However, if we make that type of revelation our end goal, we end up meeting everyone in the same place. We all become equal in understanding who Jesus is. There is nothing wrong with that; we just can't stay there!

At some point we all have to move from other people's opinions into a pure revelatory conviction that is personal.

It's a place of uniformity where all people who get there see the same thing. It's a universal revelation that qualifies us for something much greater. It becomes a launching pad to obtain a third level of revelation that nobody seems to be talking about in our churches. A level of revelation that makes us truly unique!

You see, the conversation that Jesus had with Peter shifted the focus from Him to Peter. The first two levels of revelation were all about Jesus; however, there was a third level of revelation that Jesus wanted Peter to grasp that had nothing to do with Jesus. It had everything to do with Peter.

When Peter was ready to receive it, Jesus turned to Peter and said:

> *"Peter, now that you know what other people are saying about Me, and now that you know, by revelation, who I am, it is time for you to understand something else. Let me tell you who you are! You are Peter, and on this rock I will build My church, and the gates of Hades shall not prevail against it."*

Wow, let's think about this for just a moment. For the first time in his life, Peter had a revelation about who *he* was supposed to be, as Jesus Himself identified Peter by uttering words of destiny and purpose for his personal life. He declared the very thing that made Peter unique. He called him Peter (Rock), and with those words He released a revelation of prophetic destiny over Peter's life.

This is a third-level revelation that we all need to have. It's this level of understanding that will make us all diverse. It will make us all unique. We all have to hear the same words that Peter heard that day. The only difference is that those words are unique to each individual. On this level, where it's revealed who we are on individually, the words we hear are unique to us.

When Peter heard Jesus reveal to him who he was, the gates of hell could no longer prevail.

We all need to come to a place where Jesus turns to us and says, "Now that you know what others say, and now that you know who I am, let me tell you who *you* are!"

That type of supernatural revelation will propel us into our own unique prophetic destiny that He has for us. In fact, it's this level of understanding that becomes the foundation of the church. Knowing this prophetic purpose becomes the foundation upon which the church will be built. A victorious church against which the gates of Hades can't prevail.

If we want to truly overthrow the gates of hell, we need to attain this level of revelation. This is where the action happens. On this level is where the battle is won. This is the place where everyone in God's army finds his or her lane, position, and rank. Its power is in diversity, a diversity that can only be uncovered on this third level.

What we see and discover here will more than likely be something that cannot be contained by any box that we previously were part of. The manifestation of that level of revelation requires a blank canvas. It requires undeveloped land that now can be developed in such a way that it is unique to you.

Remember the verse from the book of Romans that we read at the beginning of this book: *"For the creation waits in eager expectation for the children of God to be revealed"* (Romans 8:19, NIV).

It's in this moment, when Jesus turns to you and identifies your prophetic destiny by showing you who *you* are, that you become revealed as a son of God. In other words, if we want creation to stop waiting, we cannot accomplish that unless we get to that third-level revelation. When Peter heard Jesus reveal to him who he was, the gates of hell could no longer prevail.

When I hear the words of Jesus declaring who I am, I'm placed on a path where I now can truly become revealed as a son of God. I become part of the answer to a waiting world.

This is truly the last step of the process of being un-boxed. In this step it's no longer about the box. It's about creating something brand new. It's place where boxes are irrelevant. A place where we can create something so unique that no box can contain it. It's unique to you and who God called you to be.

- A place that can only be discovered in a place without boxes.
- A place without limitation.
- A place without predefined assumptions, boundaries and rules made by man.
- A place of tremendous freedom to truly become who you are created to be.

"Therefore if the Son makes you free, you shall be free in-deed" (John 8:36, NIV). True freedom to become who you are called to be is found on this level. You can be free indeed!

Coaching Questions

1. Are there any areas that the Lord has shown you throughout this book that you couldn't see before? What are those areas? What can you practically do to pursue those areas?

_____

_____

_____

_____

_____

_____

_____

2. In this chapter I discuss a teaching on the three levels of revelation from the life of Peter. Do you feel like you have had a third-level revelation experience? Can you explain what you feel that revelation is for you? What can you practically do to start manifesting your true identity in a purposeful way to the world around you?

chapter 10

Boxes Kill Dreams

BOXES KILL DREAMS. Boxes suffocate the vision God has for our lives. Unless we dismantle the boxes in our lives as identified through the process in this book, we will never become who we are supposed to be. It's worth it to embark on this journey into the unknown to discover what He has in store for you.

Even though it's a lonely process, you don't have to do it alone. We all are on a quest to discover who we are. Even though the end result is uniquely different for each person, we can still journey together.

We are living a boxed-up world. The church has come to believe a lie that the way we do things is the way it should always be done. Yet there is so much more, as we have discovered through the pages of this book.

In this final chapter, I would like to talk about God's dream and God's vision. As we receive His dream and His vision for our lives, as He identifies us like He did with Peter, we become really unstoppable. However, God's dream and vision is in danger of going extinct in the religious environments we, as leaders, create. We've become so accustomed to leading a certain way. We need to unlearn so many things in order to remove and destroy those boxes we've become so dependent on.

God's dream and vision is in danger of going extinct in the religious environments we, as leaders, create.

We have to change our environment to something that allows God's dream to be revealed and, ultimately, manifested in our midst. As I speak to audiences and congregations, and as I talk with people individually, I often ask the question: "What happens when God shows up in a place? What happens when His glory manifests?"

When you ask a question like that, you get all kinds of answers. You get answers like this:

- When God shows up the blind will see!
- When God shows up the lame will walk!
- When God shows up people will get saved!
- When God shows up bondage is broken!
- When God shows up even the dead will be raised!

Even though all those things are true, there is something far more profound that happens when God shows up. Let's read about it:

> *And it shall come to pass afterward*
> *That I will pour out My Spirit on all flesh;*
> *Your sons and your daughters shall prophesy,*
> *Your old men shall dream dreams,*
> *Your young men shall see visions (Joel 2:28, NKJV).*

I'm sure you've heard or read this passage many times. The danger of hearing the same thing over and over again is that you sometimes fail to see the obvious. Let's look at it again, but now in a fresh way.

In this scripture the prophet Joel talks about a time where God will pour out His Spirit on all flesh. He wants to show up for all of us. He wants His spirit to be poured out on every single individual. He wants to show up in the life of every person.

We need to develop a culture and climate where God can simply pour out His Spirit.

Then the prophet continues to explain what will happen when He shows up—something far more profound than the deaf hearing and the blind seeing. Important though those things are, what Joel is talking about here is far more powerful than that.

What can be more powerful, you ask?

When God shows up and pours out His Spirit, our old men shall dream dreams and our young men shall see visions. Let's mediate on that for a moment. That old man lost his dream many years ago. He had lost hope a long time ago. But when God shows up, that man will regain hope and dream again.

Wow!

That young man had never had a vision for his life. The world had looked at him with disgust, telling him that he'd never accomplish anything. But when God pours out His Spirit, that young man will get a vision from God! That old man's dream and young man's vision manifested will reveal the sons of God in the earth so that creation can stop waiting.

As leaders, our primary task is to facilitate an environment in the church where this process can take place. We need to develop a culture and climate where God can simply pour out His Spirit. A place where He can show up and release dreams and visions to all flesh.

Then, and only then, can we experience a church built on a foundation that is solid, where the very word of God is spoken to each and every individual and they catch a revelation of what their inheritance truly is. Isn't that powerful?

As long as we keep our world boxed up by mentalities and mind-sets that keep this process from taking place, it will keep the gates of hell fortified.

It will keep creation waiting.

It will keep us unfulfilled.

It will keep us busy, while accomplishing little.

It will keep us from truly becoming who we are supposed to be in the earth.

We can't afford to do that. Not for ourselves, but also not for those we are called to.

God's Dream

Before I close this message, I want to share one more thing about "God's dream." God's dream is powerful. It has the ability to leave a lasting impact on creation as it manifests in the earth. However, as long as we look at God's dream in a "boxed" mind-set we will never be able to see it, let alone live it!

When God gives you a dream, chances are that the people around you, especially those close to you, will not understand what it is you are seeing.

Here is the story of a man who had a dream from God:

Now Joseph had a dream, and he told it to his brothers; and they hated him even more. So he said to them, "Please hear this dream which I have dreamed: There we were, binding sheaves in the field. Then behold, my sheaf arose and also stood upright; and indeed your sheaves stood all around and bowed down to my sheaf." And his brothers said to him, "Shall you indeed reign over us? Or shall you indeed have dominion over us?" So they hated him even more for his dreams and for his words.

Then he dreamed still another dream and told it to his brothers, and said, "Look, I have dreamed another dream. And this time, the sun, the moon, and the eleven stars bowed down to me." So he told it to his father and his brothers; and his father rebuked him and said to him, "What is this dream that you have dreamed? Shall your mother and I and your brothers indeed come to bow down to the earth before you?" And his brothers envied him, but his father kept the matter in mind. (Genesis 37:5-11, NKJV).

Joseph had two dreams that he shared with his family. Both his parents and his brothers listened to what Joseph had to say, but they were not amused—to say the least. When God gives you a dream, chances are that the people around you, especially those close to you, will not understand what it is you are seeing.

In both these dreams, Joseph describes a scenario where both his brothers and his parents bow for him. In the first dream he sees a sheaf in the field that belonged to him, as well as other sheaves that belonged to his brothers. The sheaves of the brothers ended up bowing to Joseph's sheaf.

Then Joseph continues to share his second dream. In that dream, eleven stars, as well as the sun and the moon, bowed before Joseph. While sharing this dream, it was implied that his father, mother, and brothers would end up bowing before Joseph. As a result, his brothers envied him and hated him even more!

When His presence is there, we automatically bow down.

I can sort of understand their reaction. What was Joseph thinking? Saying that he was more important than his family. What Kool-Aid did he drink that made him believe they would all bow to him?

However, when we look at this on a deeper level there is actually a lesson to learn. Throughout the Bible we read stories of God showing up for people in different places. For example, remember when the commander of the army of the Lord showed up for Joshua? It says that *"Joshua fell on his face to the earth and worshipped"* (Joshua 5:14).

Whenever God manifests himself it makes people fall to their faces. His presence demands that we bow down. When His presence is there, we automatically bow down. You'll see it throughout the whole Bible, from Genesis to Revelation.

Now let's go back to God's dream for our lives. When He gives us a dream or when He gives us a vision something profound happens. He starts showing up through that dream. He will manifest His presence through that dream and through that vision.

Why? Because the dream and vision originated from the heart of God. Now that we catch the dream and vision and start to walk in it, He will actually start manifesting through our lives. And when He manifests, everything bows down.

That's the power of God's dream. It demands for everything and everyone to bow down. And that's a good thing. Because the dream is God's. We want people to encounter God through the dreams and vision He has given us.

In Joseph's case there was a problem. He understood this principle. He knew that as he dreamed the dream of God that everything would bow to that dream. Yet his brothers didn't understand it. They became filled with envy and hatred. They couldn't separate God's dream from Joseph the person.

They lived in a paradigm, or box, that limited them to seeing what Joseph was able to see all along. They couldn't see the reality that *they too* could have a dream. That they too, had a prophetic destiny. Because they couldn't see that, they despised Joseph. *What made him so special that he could rule over them?* they wondered.

Joseph's brothers couldn't separate God's dream from Joseph the person.

Isn't this same thing true in our reality so often? We somehow believe that there is only one who can have a dream. We sometimes believe there can be only one vision and that we all must support that one vision. In our churches we talk about "the vision of the house" as if there were only one vision for us all to follow, one dream for us all to bow to.

Yet, God wants to pour out His Spirit on all flesh. He wants to give us all a dream. He wants to give vision to all.

Joseph's brothers failed to understand that. They assumed there could be only one leader. The box in their mind that kept them from seeing the bigger picture caused them to despise the very thing that originated from the heart of God. The truth was that God had a dream for all of them. Each individual in that group that day was destined with his own unique prophetic purpose.

If we read several chapters further, we even see that Jacob finally sees the plurality of vision that God had prepared for each of them. In Genesis 49, just before Jacob dies, he prophesies and declares God's vision for each of his sons.

God didn't have a dream and vision for just Joseph. He had a vision for all of them. They somehow failed to see that reality, which caused them to despise the very thing God initiated. They should have realized that, in fact, they could have a dream too. That God wanted to manifest Himself through the brothers just as much as He would manifest Himself through Joseph.

They should have realized that as God showed up through their dreams that Joseph would have gladly bowed down to His presence, as He would become revealed through those dreams as well. This is what we can learn from it:

- God pours out His spirit on all flesh.
- Nobody has exclusive rights to the dream of God. He wants to give a dream to all individuals.

Collectively, as we start walking out that dream, we will bow to each other as we see God manifested through each and every one of us. I will bow to you and your dream as you bow to me and my dream. The brothers failed to see this, but we will learn from it.

We will all dream big. We will all support each other. We will destroy all boxes that stand in the way of this.

Today, we'll start to DREAM BIG!

Coaching Questions

Please write down your overall takeaways, action steps and new insight that you gained throughout this book.

_____

_____

_____

_____

_____

_____

_____

_____

Additional Words from the Author

IF YOU MADE IT TO THIS PAGE, then it probably means the message of *Unboxed: Uncovering New Paradigms* resonated with you. But before you put the book away, I want to share some additional thoughts with you. (Don't worry—I won't be long.)

My hope is that the message you've just read has given you the ability and courage to dream far beyond your current reality. God is able—and willing—to give you much more than what you can even dream of or imagine (Eph. 3:20). My prayer for you is that you have caught a glimpse of that truth from looking into the pages of this book.

Personal Stories Reveal a Personal Journey

Before publishing *Unboxed*, I distributed the finished manuscript to about 50 people who are close to my heart and whose feedback I respect. Many of them contributed endorsements, which you read at the beginning of the book. I received some great feedback from them that I ended up integrating into the final version of *Unboxed*. One suggestion made repeatedly was that I should include "coaching questions" after each chapter, which I ended up doing in the final product.

Also, an observation made by several people was that I used a lot of personal stories at the beginning of the book but reduced the number toward the end of the book. I realized they were right. Why did I reduce the use of personal stories? I wondered. Indeed, the further you get in the book, the more abstract and conceptual the content becomes. It was suggested that I should continue the use of personal stories all the way through.

I thought about that, prayed about it, and even talked with some friends about it. Through this process I came to realize that even though I wrote in prophetic, revelatory, and conceptual language, the book is actually very personal, even without my own stories. I lived (and am living) through each aspect, each phase of getting unboxed, as described in each chapter. *Unboxed* is literally the result of a 20-year personal journey put into writing.

In fact, this message is so much a part of me that I was able to write *Unboxed*, for the most part, in one weekend. Because it had been in me so long it was easy to give birth to it, fast. During the process I realized the Lord had me write this book for such a time as this to be a clarion call to the church to think bigger and beyond. Writing it was so natural for me, and I felt the Holy Spirit's anointing as I developed each chapter. Why, then, did I reduce the use of personal stories as I got further into the writing?

My Path Isn't a Roadmap

This is what I believe is the reason: The whole point of the *Unboxed* message is that we need to move away from established paradigms so God can speak to us in new ways that will enable us to journey into the future to discover uncharted territories that He has prepared for us alone. Using too many personal stories and examples of how God led me on my journey poses a risk that others will think they should model their experience after mine. Believe me, I have seen this happen many times.

The power of a personal testimony, and the journey and decisions I had to make, have the potential to create the very thing we don't want—a new box.

When I say, "This is what God did in my life, and these are the decisions I had to make to see these specific results," there is a temptation for others to simply repeat the "formula" to get the same results. By sharing too many personal stories I could have conditioned my readers to embrace a "new set of rules" as the answer for their own situations.

What's unboxed for me might not be unboxed for you. We each have our own journey to make. We each have our own unconventional decisions to make. God speaks to each of us in different ways. In fact, He may instruct two individuals to do opposite things in similar situations, but in each case His objective is to get them both unboxed. I don't want my personal story to become your roadmap to becoming unboxed. You need to create your own story. You need to trail-blaze your own path to greatness.

Unboxed: Like a Priceless Pearl

Even though the unboxing process never ends, as there are always more layers to peel back from our conditioned lives,

I can say this: I am right now living the live I always wanted to live and much, much more.

Many of the prophetic words spoken over my life have actually come to pass. In not just one area of my life, but across many areas, I've seen God take me to places I couldn't have imagined I would ever get to.

On a ministry level he has connected me on a level of authority and influence that is incredible. My family life is amazing, and my kids all are living their own out-of-the-box Spirit-led lives in their own ways.

I have experienced incredible financial abundance. I own several businesses that have been blessed beyond what I ever thought was possible. And most of all, I feel like I'm living out my prophetic destiny in a nondualistic, powerful way.

Having that said, I can truly say with absolute certainty that the blessings I've reaped throughout my life are the result of the very process I've described in this book. This journey is not for the faint of heart. It takes courage to innovate, create something new, and follow the Lord's direction. Getting unboxed required me to make unconventional decisions, say no to family expectations, burn bridges, take tremendous risks, die daily to self, say yes when everyone else was saying no, challenge the status quo, and deep-dive into the unknown regularly.

It hasn't always been easy (and still isn't at times), but the destination is well worth the journey. You'll be challenged and experience opposition—often from people you least expect (or want) to oppose you. The reward, however, is amazing! The impact on the world around you is worth it all.

In Matthew 13:45-46, Jesus said that when the merchant who was looking for fine pearls found the one of great value, he sold all he had and bought it. Find that pearl the merchant found. For, once you do, it will be worth risking all to have it!

NOTES